LET HER SPEAK

LET HER SPEAK

Transcript of Texas State Senator Wendy Davis's June 25, 2013, Filibuster of the Texas State Senate

COUNTERPATH   DENVER   2013

Counterpath
Denver, Colorado
www.counterpathpress.org

Library of Congress Cataloging-in-Publication Data
is available from the publisher.

NOTE ON THE TRANSCRIPTION

This transcription is based on the video of the June 25, 2013, session of the Texas State Senate posted on the Texas State Senate website. It was initially compiled by Workers via Amazon Mechanical Turk, with particular thanks to Ashley Pound.

Senator Davis: Yes, Mr. President. I intend to speak for an extended period of time on the bill. Thank you very much.

Thank you, Mr. President and thank you members. As we began to debate this bill on the senate floor last week, we talked about the fact that we were here on this particular motion because we had taken extraordinary measures to be here, and I want to talk about that for a moment, how we wound up at this moment, on this day, on the senate floor, debating this bill. And we wound up here because extraordinary measures were taken in order to assure that we would land here. We all know that the bills that are before us today, that have been folded into this one bill, Senate Bill 5, are bills that were filed during the regular called session of the Texas Legislature, and we all know, as a body, why we did not hear this bill during the regular session. And that is because, of course, under our rules, our traditions, it takes two-thirds of the members of this body in order to suspend the regular order of business, because it is typical for a blocker bill to be filed, in order for a bill to be taken up. And we know that there were eleven members of this body who refused to allow the suspension of that particular rule. We know that there were no real courses of action on the house fight on this bill during the regular session as well. And when the session ended, and within the hour, Governor Perry called us back, he initially called us back for another matter that also could not be heard on this senate floor during the regular session because of that two-thirds rule, and of course that was our redistricting bills. And now something extraordinary has happened; we were called to a special session, our presiding officer, has decided against tradition of the Texas Senate to have us convene in order to talk about bills that could not be taken up in the regular session and to not follow the tradition of the two-thirds rule in order to accommodate that occurring.

This bill, of course, is one that impacts many, many people. And it's one that took extraordinary measures in order for us to be here and to converse on it today. Members, I'm rising on the floor today to humbly give voice to thousands of Texans who have been ignored. These are Texans who relied on the minority members of this senate in order for their voices to be heard. These voices have been silenced by a governor who made blind partisanship and personal political ambition the official business of our great state. And sadly he's being abetted by legislative leaders who either share this blind partisanship, or simply do not have the strength to oppose it. Partisanship and ambition are not unusual in the state capital, but here in Texas, right now, it has risen to a level of profound irresponsibility and the raw abuse of power. The actions intended by our state leaders on this particular bill hurt Texans. There is no doubt about that. They hurt women; they hurt their families. The actions in this bill undermine the hard work and commitment of fair-minded, mainstream, Texas families, who want nothing more than to work hard, raise their children, stay healthy and be a productive part of the greatest state in our country. These mainstream Texas families embrace the challenge to create the greatest possible Texas. Yet, they are pushed back and they're held down by narrow and divisive interests that are driving our state, and this bill is an example of that narrow partisanship.

Today I'm going to talk about the paths these leaders have chosen under this bill and the dark place that the bill will take us. I will try to explain the history of the failed legislation before us, the impact of that legislation, and most importantly what history tells us about these policies and the motivations behind them. They do real damage to our state and to the families whose rights are violated, and whose personal relationship with their doctor and their creator, which should belong to them and them alone, are being violated. Most importantly today I will share with you what thousands of families have had to say about this legislation and those bringing this legislation to the floor, when the majority of Texans want us working to press upon genuine business of the state of Texas.

The legislation before you has a history, as we talked about a moment ago and I'm going to go specifically through the history of this particular bill. There was ample opportunity during the special sessions to move theses pieces of legislation and some did move, but the will of the legislature did not propel them timely through the process. And here are the basics about what happened to each of those. SB 25 by Senator Hegar was the 20 week abortion bill, filed on March the 5th. It was referred to state affairs on March the 12th; it never received a senate hearing. The house companion, House Bill 2364, by Representative Laubenberg, was filed on March the 5th, referred to state affairs on March the 11th. A hearing was held on April 10th. It was reported out of house state affairs on May the 2nd. The bill was sent to house calendars on May 7th, and it was never placed on the calendar. SB 97, by Senator Patrick, regarding abortion inducing drugs and regulations on the administration of those drugs, was filed on November the twelfth, it was referred to health and human services on January 28th and the senate hearing was held on February 26th. It was reported out of the senate health and human service committee on March 28th but it died on the senate intent's calendar, and it died for the reason that I mentioned a moment ago, because a third of the members of this senate, who represented voices who deserve to be heard, prevented the bill from coming forward. There was no house companion to that bill. SB 537, by Senator Deuell, related to the regulation of abortion facilities requiring that they all have a standard met for ambulatory surgical centers. That bill was filed on February 13th. It was referred to health and human services on March 19th, excuse me, February 20th. There was a senate hearing on the bill March 19th. It was reported out of committee on March 26th and it died on the senate intent calendar. Again, it died because a third of the members of this body made it so. There was no house companion filed to that bill. SB 1198, by Senator Taylor, relating to hospital admitting privileges and the requirement that doctors who perform abortions have admitting privileges at a hospital within a certain distance. It was filed on March the sixth; it was referred to health and human services committee on March the twelfth. The senate hearing was held on April the 16th. It was reported out of committee on April 22nd and it died on the senate intent calendar for the reasons that I mentioned a moment ago, because the minority group of senators, who represent voices across the state of Texas, made it so. There was a house companion to that bill. HB 2816, by Representative Burkett. It was filed on March the seventh. It was referred to house state affairs on March 18th, the house hearing was held on March 27th. It was reported out of committee on April 24th, and sent to house calendars on April 26th, where it died.

And how did we get here? Well, of course we were called to a special session, and as I said, that session did not begin with the addition of this bill, it began with redistricting. On June the 10th, Governor Perry added transportation funding to the call, and of course, the Democrats in this chamber had indicated our intention that we would vote to advance that bill were it placed before this one today. We understand that transportation is a priority. On June the eleventh, these bills were filed, several bills were filed, um, including also a bill by Senator Huffman, SB 23, a bill again that the Democrats have indicated were it taken up today, before this bill, we would have joined our colleagues in passing it because we believe it's important. Governor Perry, of course, on that day also expanded the special session to include legislation relating to the regulation of abortion procedures, providers and facilities. He also spoke, in support of that call, about the horrors of The National Late Term Abortion Industry. He said that sadly some of those atrocities happen in our own state. And in Texas we value all life and we've worked to cultivate a culture that supports the birth of every child. He said that we have an obligation to protect unborn children and to hold those who peddle abortions to standards that would minimize the death, disease, and pain that they cause. What he did not do was place on the call anything that would help to prevent unplanned pregnancy. What he did not do is place anything on the call that would aid women in making sure they never find themselves in need of the occasion that we meet here today to discuss. On that same day the call was broadened again. The bills were referred and put on a fast track for a hearing the following day, living—leaving little to no advance notice for a public hearing. But fortunately a procedural action forced the committee to wait an extra day; a tagging of the bill, allowing more Texans the opportunity to have their voices heard on these issues. Ultimately, the Republican leadership agreed to move only one bill on the senate floor and that was SB 5 that is before us today. Before bringing the bill up there was discussion amongst the majority and the 20 week fetal pain portion of the bill was removed by Republicans before the bill was presented to us for our consideration on the floor. As you probably remember from that night, Democratic senators offered seventeen amendments to the bill on the senate floor to address concerns from stakeholders, primarily to address concerns, again, that prevention of abortion is the surest way . . . excuse me, that prevention of pregnancy is the surest way to decrease the demand for abortion. Included in those amendments were a request that we accept Medicaid funding from the federal level, which we knew would bring down a tremendous amount of money and assistance for women's health. Included in that was a full funding of the Women's Health Program which provides a ninety to ten match for uses of helping women who are in need of family planning services. But all of those amendments were rejected. The bill was voted out on party lines and then moved over to the house. The bill was received by the house on June 20th and was set for a public hearing the following day. The hearing also included HB 16 which was the 20-week stand alone bill and HB 60, the omnibus bill. Hundreds of Texans from all over the state appeared to testify at the hearing, but unfortunately the hearing, which lasted sometime until the wee hours of the morning, 3:30 to 4 o'clock, was halted before all of the testimony was given by those who had waited, many of them from the prior morning, to voice their feelings on the bill. And it is my intention today to give them a voice by reading all of their testimonies on the senate floor. In committee SB 5 was changed to include the section of the bill, the 20-week ban, that was removed in the senate: also, HB 60 and HB 61. On the house floor there was minimal engagement and participation by the house author on the legislation. House D's offered thirteen amendments targeted at addressing concerns raised by stake-holders. All were rejected. And now, we find ourselves here.

This is the omnibus piece of legislation that contains these elements of bills that were filed in the 83rd session: the 20-week ban, the abortion inducing drugs provision, the ambulatory surgical center standards, and the hospital admitting privileges. The alleged reason for the bill is to enhance patient safety. But what they really do is create provisions that treat women as though they are not capable of making their own medical decisions. They weaken standards of care because as we all know, every member on this floor knows that the provisions of the ambulatory surgical center standards will immediately place 37 of the 42 abortion clinics in Texas out of compliance. And though the arguments on the senate floor were made that the reason for those standards was for patient safety, not a single instance, not a single instance, could be demonstrated to illustrate why those ambulatory surgical standards were important in assuring women's safety. Not a single example was provided where women had been provided a less safe atmosphere in the existing clinical setting today than they would receive in that setting. What this bill really does, is to threaten the doctor-patient relationship, and we know that we received a great deal of information from doctors' groups which I'll read into the record in a little while about the intrusion on that relationship and we know that in no other instance has this legislature chosen to place itself between a woman and her doctor, or any patient and their doctor. We know that these additional standards are unnecessary. They're unsupported by scientific evidence, including unnecessary requirements that may be extremely difficult and in some cases impossible to meet without a basis in public health or safety.

As we've been debating this issue, we have been reminded that there was a time in our country when only the wealthy could afford to access abortion services because they had the ability to travel to places that it was legal, and that women who didn't have that access to care were relegated either to carrying a pregnancy to term or, and very sadly, to some unsafe methods that they turned to, to try to address that need. And we know that women lost their lives over that. We also know, in written testimony from the group, The National Obstetrics and Gynecologic Group, that their fear is the same thing is going to happen. In the state of Texas, through this bill, we are asking that women be forced to step back in history, back to a time when once again wealthy women who have the ability and the flexibility in their lives and their schedules to travel for these services will be accommodated, and women who will not, will suffer a different and unfortunately, probably in some instances, a life-threatening consequence.

The 20-week ban on abortion, we've heard a great deal of testimony about that particular provision and I want to hit a few highlights of what has been shared with us. Number one, and most importantly, from our medical community we've heard the concern that this interferes with the practice of medicine. As important, we know that concerns have been raised that this ban interferes with a woman's healthcare decision before she and her doctor may have important health information about her own health and the health of the pregnancy. The ban will have devastating consequences when a woman is experiencing medical complications, and unfortunately it bans abortion before a woman may receive important information about her own health and the health of her pregnancy. Fewer than two percent of abortions occur after 20 weeks and while they are uncommon, it is important that a woman and her doctor have every medical option available. On the abortion inducing drugs restrictions, some of the key concerns that we have had—heard about that: one, that it requires that the physician preferred course of treatment be replaced with a treatment that is potentially more physically harmful to the patient, and again, though asked, no on this senate floor was able to provide information to us that demonstrated any other incidents where the legislature had taken it upon itself to interfere in such a dramatic way in a physician's decision-making as it pertains to the administration of treatment. The bill would require physicians to follow an outdated protocol, limiting women's access to safe, effective, medication abortion. It directly contradicts a physician's ability to provide the highest level of care for their patients by requiring a government prescribed course of treatment. It prohibits—prohibits physicians in Texas from providing the standard of care to their patients, subjecting physicians to disciplinary action for providing the nationally recognized standard of care endorsed by the leading medical professional association of obstetrician and gynecologists, ACOG. On the ambulatory surgical center standards, additional state government regulation on an already heavily regulated practice of medicine was one of the primary concerns raised there. Healthcare providers comply that all federal, state, and local laws and regulations, and they strongly opposed regulations that failed to make healthcare more cost effective, safer, efficient, or accessible. Texas already requires abortions performed after 16 weeks to be performed in ambulatory surgical centers. And we know, and I'll read some information in a little while about the fact, that there is a reason for that, because the incidents of problems that arise prior to that period of time at existing clinical settings is extremely low. Much lower, in fact, than any complications that arise from the live births, of which we are not subjecting to the same standards. When these facilities close, and they will, women will lose access to their trusted provider. These closed facilities cannot offer any other services that they may have been providing. And we know that in Texas sometimes these facilities are shared facilities where family planning services are also provided.

What is required of reproductive healthcare centers today? Today in the United States, reproductive healthcare services are among the safest and most commonly sought forms of care in the United States. Placing unreasonable requirements on healthcare centers that provide safe, legal abortions today is uncalled for, and again, not a hint of evidence has been offered as to why it's needed. And we know why. Governor Dewhurst's Tweet told us why. It is because the real aim of this bill is not to make women safer but it is to force the closure of multiple facilities across the state of Texas without a single care or concern for the women whose lives will be impacted by that decision. Not a single care or concern. Because our leadership has demonstrated that it is prioritizing its own political possibilities over potential and devastating consequences for individual women.

Let's talk about the parts of the bill that are medically unnecessary. First of all, I think each of us would agree that as patients we trust our doctors, not the government, to determine what medical equipment and what sized room is necessary to provide us with good care. It is medically unnecessary to require health centers to build a hospital-grade operating room for an abortion procedure when one is not required for this type of procedure. And in fact, we know there are many outpatient clinical procedures that are more invasive, have higher incidences of problems, that today are allowed to take place in clinical settings such as doctor's office without the standards that are being required in this bill. Texas, of course, as I said a moment ago, already requires that abortions performed after 16 weeks be performed at ambulatory surgical centers. This provision, the provision in these bills, goes further by requiring that all health centers that provide abortions comply with regulations that are equivalent to the governing places where surgery takes place. The vast majority of abortions, however, are outpatient procedures that can be performed in a health center, making those requirements inappropriate, unnecessary, and not at all about the health of women.

I want to read into the record written testimony that we were provided by a variety of groups on the measures that are before us today. This from the Texas Medical Association, it was addressed to the health committee on state affairs on health bill 16 and sixty, by Representative Jody Laubenberg, and it's dated June the twentieth, 2013.

"The Texas Medical Association is a private, voluntary, nonprofit, association of more than 47,000 member physicians and medical students. TMA. was funded in 1853 to serve the people of Texas in matters of medical care, prevention, and cure of disease, and improvement of public health. Today our maxim continues in the same directions: physicians caring for Texans. TMA's diverse physician members practice in all fields of medical specialization. Our member physicians fall on both sides of any debate on abortion. Our concerns with house bill thirteen and sixty are not based on any position on abortion, rather our concerns are with legislative intrusion into the patient's physician relationship and the details of the practice of medicine and with a legislatively created standard of care. Examples of concerns of these proposed bills are House Bill 60's, section 3, Sub chapter D, directs physicians to take specific action related to the prescription of an abortion inducing drug, approved by the U.S. Food and Drug Administration for use by women who seek an abortion. The bill prescribes details in the practice of medicine such as requirements for the examination, patient-physician communications, and protocols. As previously outlined in our written statement on senate bill 97, in the 83rd Texas Legislature, TMA is concerned this legislation sets a dangerous precedent of the legislature prescribing the details of the practice of medicine. The medical community, based on science, must make these determinations, not the legislature. Sections 171.0031 and 171.063C and HB 60 would require a physician or other healthcare personnel to be available by phone 24 hours a day indefinitely. Although the intent of these provisions may be to allow the patient access to the provider for assistance with complications, as written they are overly broad, and could require 24/7 access for years. Furthermore, these sections are vague in that they appear to require access to medical records 24 hours a day, which is an overly broad an unprecedented requirement. House Bill 16, section two, sub chapter C, and House Bill 60, section three, sub chapter C, included a definition of profound and irremediable congenital anomaly based on the amount of time a physician reasonably believes the infant would survive after birth. The definition places that time at minutes to hours, which TMA opposes, because it is arbitrary and would be impossible for a physician to predict. The bill may seek to allow an exception for conditions in which death after birth would be imminent and in that regard use of the word 'imminent' would be more appropriate than minutes to hours. Additionally, this proposed definition does not take into account fetal trauma which in severe situations, could result in imminent death after birth. The following definition for severe fetal abnormality currently exists in section 285.202 health and safety code and may be an appropriate definition to replace the proposed definition for profound and irremediable congenital anomaly to severe fetal abnormality, meaning a life-threatening physical condition that in reasonable medical judgment, regardless of the provision of life-saving medical treatment, is incompatible with life outside the womb. The patient-physician relationship is one of mutuality and trust. Patients must be able to trust that their physicians are always acting in each patient's individual best interest and must be assured of candid communication with their physician so they may effectively evaluate their medical care options. TMA strongly opposes any legislation that interferes in this relationship. TMA appreciates the opportunity to provide you our concerns regarding HBs 16 and sixty and urges you to take these comments into serious consideration. We are happy to provide any additional information or assistance you may request," and it is signed by Steven Brotherton, M.D., the president of TMA

We also have written testimony provided to the health and human services committee by Robin Wallace, M.D.M.A.S., who is a leadership training academy fellow with physicians for reproductive health. She testified before the Texas Senate committee on health and human services on Senate Bill 537 during a regular session on March 19th, 2013 and she provided this written testimony, which I think is compelling.

"Physicians for reproductive health is a doctor-led national advocacy organization that uses evidence-based medicine to promote sound reproductive health policies. We work to make quality reproductive health services an integral part of women's healthcare. Physicians for reproductive health opposes Senate Bill 537 which would impose burdensome, expensive, and unnecessary requirements on facilities providing surgical abortions in Texas, causing many to shut down. Though this bill purports to improve patient safety, it would in fact harm women by reducing access to safe, timely abortion services. I am a board certified family medicine doctor licensed to practice medicine in Texas. I received my medical degree from the University of North Carolina in Chapel Hill. I completed my post-graduate training at the Santa Rosa Family Medicine Residency, an affiliate of the University of California, San Francisco. I also completed a fellowship in primary care research in family planning at UCSF as one of a select number of family physicians who have participated in this specialty training. I currently live and practice in the Dallas-Fort Worth area. I am pleased to submit this testimony and opposition to SB 537 on behalf of physicians for reproductive health. SB 537 is harmful to women. As a physician who takes care of women every single day, I cannot stress enough how dangerous these laws are to the health and well-being of my patients. Women need timely access to safe abortion care. SB 537 imposes medically unnecessary standards on abortion facilities. SB 537 would require abortion facilities to become ambulatory surgical centers (ACSs), which are the setting for complicated and invasive surgical procedures. Abortion, especially early abortion, in the first twelve weeks, is a safe medical procedure with inherently low-risk in outpatient settings without hospital-like facilities. Serious complications arising from surgical abortions at any gestational age are uncommon. By comparison, pregnancy and childbirth are significantly more dangerous to women than abortion. For example, CDC data indicates that the pregnancy related mortality ratio in the United States is 15.2 deaths per 100,000 live births compared to 0.64 deaths per 100,000 legal abortions," and she provides a footnote for that from the CDC, in a report that was compiled in 2011. "The requirements imposed by this bill are simply medically unnecessary, unsupported by scientific evidence, and contrary to the standards of care." She goes on to say, "I think of my patient, Samantha, a mother of a two-year old son, who was born two months early. Upon determining that she was pregnant again, Samantha was overwhelmed by the thought of another pregnancy with a potential risk of complications and she decided to terminate that pregnancy. Luckily, Samantha lived within fifteen miles of our outpatient clinic, which was easily accessible on a major city bus route. Samantha was able to have her abortion safely and timely in the first trimester. Another patient named Monica, a 20-three year old woman, presented me at almost twelve weeks; she had a three and half month old baby girl at home who was delivered by cesarean section. This patient did not realize she was pregnant earlier because she had not had a menstrual period since her delivery. We were able to provide her abortion procedure to her safely and quickly so that she could return home to care for her baby. A young mother does not have time to travel many miles or hours away. She needs to be able to get back to her infant and take care of herself and her family. My patients come from all walks of life, from every situation imaginable. One thing they have in common is that they seek abortion because they've weighed all the options and know in their hearts that this private decision is best for themselves and their families. They do not deserve the burden of a law that has no medical benefits or basis. If SB 537 becomes law, I fear for my patients like Samantha and Monica, who already face challenges receiving abortion care in Texas. The cost prohibitive regulations associated with SB 537 would force safe, accessible, abortion facilities to close while doing nothing to improve patient safety. SB 537 would deny women safe, needed, medical care. SB 537 would create unreasonable obstacles for healthcare providers like myself who are committed to protecting the health of women by making these needed services available. Many health centers would close due to the inability to comply with the standards of an ASC. In turn this would force women and Texans to travel out of state, if they have the resources, or would deny them safe care all together. I cared for a patient, Julia, a registered nurse with a young child at home. Julia was pregnant and this was a very wanted pregnancy. She and her husband discovered through a routine 14-week ultrasound that she had a very high-risk pregnancy with a significant chance of still-birth. They made the difficult decision to end the pregnancy. We were the closest provider to Julia, but still a 4-hour bus ride away. Due to current Texas state law, she had to make this trip twice. Once for her required ultrasound and again after the mandatory 24-hour waiting period to have her procedure performed. Another patient of mine drove 5 hours by herself because there was no provider closer to her. Her pregnancy was diagnosed at 22 weeks with a lethal fetal anomaly. Continuing the pregnancy would mean waiting for the fetus to die in utero during labor or immediately after delivery. My patient and her husband made the heartbreaking decision to end the pregnancy. She had to stay alone at her hotel until her husband could follow 2 days later for the final day of her procedure. I provided care for her and she did medically well, but she experienced financial hardship associated with traveling such a long distance to receive care. As a physician, I know that access to safe and legal abortion care is critical to the health of women. When abortion becomes less accessible, it becomes less safe. Medically unnecessary restrictions on abortion cause women to delay their care as they locate a provider, travel greater distances, or even seek services of an unlicensed provider, all resulting in taking unnecessary risks with their health. While Texas women have the right to safe, legal abortion, in reality there are already very few facilities in Texas to provide this essential care. In 2008, 92 percent of Texas counties had no abortion provider." And she sites for that a report prepared by the Alan Guttmaucher Institute state facts about abortion available online and last accessed, according to her footnote, March 15th, 2013. "Decreasing the number of providers in Texas will have negative effects on women, even beyond the immediate outcomes of their pregnancies. Recent research has shown that when a woman seeking an abortion is denied access to care she is more likely in the future to become unemployed, live below the poverty line, and experience intimate partner violence." And she cites for that statement, Green Foster, "reports on the so few economic consequences of abortion compared to unwanted births" and she also cites, K.S. Chiver, "receiving versus being denied an abortion and subsequent experiences of intimate partner violence" in support of her statement. "If additional facilities are forced to close under the burden of SB 537, this would have a devastating impact on the health and well being of Texas women and their families. Conclusion: SB 537 does nothing to improve patient safety. Rather it would close the doors on many clinics that provide comprehensive, safe, legal, and compassionate care to women in Texas. On behalf of physicians for reproductive health I strongly urge the senate health and human services committee to oppose SB 537 and protect Texas women's health."

We also received this written testimony from the Texas Hospital Association regarding admitting privileges and this was provided on June 20th, 2013. This was testimony given in opposition to section 2, of House Bill 60, as filed by Representative Laubenberg, relating to the regulation of abortion procedures, providers, and facilities and given to the house committee on state affairs, June 20th, 2013.

"The Texas Hospital Association on behalf of its 450 member hospitals offers the following statement in opposition to section 2 of House Bill 60 as filed. Number one, hospitals should not be required to grant privileges to physicians who do not practice in a hospital. T.H.A. agrees that women should receive high quality care and that physicians should be held accountable for acts that violate their license. However, a requirement that physicians who perform one particular outpatient procedure, abortion, be privileged at a hospital is not the appropriate way to accomplish these goals. A hospital's granting privileges to a physician serves to assure the hospital that the physician has the appropriate qualifications to provide services to patients in the hospital. Thousands of physicians operate clinics and provide services in those clinics but do not have hospital admitting privileges. Requiring a hospital to grant admitting privileges to physicians who do not provide services inside the hospital is time-consuming and expensive for the hospital and does not serve the purpose for which privileges were intended. Rather, the Texas medical board is the appropriate agency to address whether physicians are delivering appropriate care to patients, as the T.M.B. regulates all physicians. Hospitals should not be required to assume responsibility for the qualifications of physicians who do not practice in the hospital. Should a woman develop complications from an abortion or any other procedure performed outside the hospital and need emergency care, she should present to a hospital emergency department. Requiring that a doctor have privileges at a particular hospital does not guarantee that this physician will be at the hospital when the woman arrives. She will appropriately be treated by the physicians staffing the emergency room when she presents there. If the emergency room physician needs to consult with the physician who performed the abortion, the treating physician can contact the doctor telephonically, which is often done in other emergency situations. Thus, T.H.A. respectfully requests that the language in proposed Section 171.0031, Section A1, be deleted. As the language in Section 171.0031, Section A2 is the best and most appropriate way to ensure that a woman who experiences complications from an abortion can get advice about and treatment of those complications. Section 171.0031-A2 requires that the physician performing the abortion provide to the patient the following: a 24/7, 365 day a week, day a year, line for her to be able to contact the physician or physician's office, the name and contact information of the hospital nearest to her home, as the woman will seek hospital services through the emergency department. Additionally, Section 245.023 of the Texas Health and Safety Code, requires the Texas Department of State Health Services, the licensing agency for abortion facilities, to maintain a toll free number for which individuals can learn, among other things, whether an administrative or civil penalty has been imposed against the facility or a physician who provides services at the facility, whether professional discipline has been imposed against a physician who provides services at the facility, and whether there are any criminal convictions on the facility or of a physician who provides services at the facility that is relevant to services provided at the facility. A copy of Section 245.023 in the implementing regulation are attached as Appendix A. They also provided a proposed an alternative amendment in alternative language: As an alternative to the deletion of Section 171.0031-A1, T.H.A. requests that new sub-section C be added to Section 171.0031 to clarify that hospitals are not required to consider or grant medical staff privileges to physicians who perform elective abortions. To begin the process of privileging, a physician submits an application to a hospital for membership on the medical staff and a request for clinical privileging. The hospital is required to review any application received and take action on it within specified timelines. Failure of the hospital to review the application or reject it without review could be grounds for a discrimination lawsuit against the hospital. To require hospitals to consider applications for medical staff membership and privileges from a physician to perform abortions will impose unnecessary administrative costs on hospitals and may subject hospitals to legal challenges if an application for membership and privileges is denied because a physician performs elective abortions. A copy of T.H.A.'s recommended amendment to section 171.0031 is attached. The attachment reads: Appendix A, Section 245.023, public information, toll free telephone number; a) the department on request shall make the following information available to the public: 1) the status of the license of the abortion facility; 2) the date of the last inspection of the facility, any violations discovered during that inspection that would pose a health risk to a patient at the facility, any challenge raised by the facility to the allegation that there was a violation, and any corrective action that is acceptable to the department and that is being undertaken by the facility with respect to the violation, and 3) an administrative or civil penalty imposed against the facility or a physician who provides services at the facility, professional discipline imposed against a physician who provides services at the facility and any criminal convictions of the facility or a physician who provides services at the facility that is relevant to services provided at the facility. Subsection B: Subsection A does not require the department to provide information that is not in the possession of the department. The Texas State Board of Medical Examiners shall provide to the department information in the possession of the board that the department is required to provide under Subsection A. The department shall maintain a toll free telephone number that a person may call to obtain the information described by Subsection A. An abortion facility shall provide to a woman at the time the woman initially consults the facility a written statement indicating the number of the toll free telephone line, maintained under Subsection C. The written statement must be available . . . is . . . must be available in English and Spanish and be in substantially the following form: a toll free telephone number, you have a right to access certain information concerning this abortion facility by using the toll free telephone number listed above. If you make a call to the number, your identity will remain anonymous. The toll free telephone line can provide you with the following information: 1) whether this abortion facility is licensed by the Texas Department of Health; 2) the date of the last inspection of this facility by the Texas Department of Health and any violations of law or rules discovered during that inspection that may pose a health risk to you; 3) any relevant fine, penalty or judgment rendered against this facility or a doctor who provides services at this facility. This section does not authorize the release of the name, address, or phone number of any employee or patient of an abortion facility or of a physician who provides services at an abortion facility."

And then this statement, by the American Congress of Obstetricians and Gynecologists: "Texas ACOG Statement Opposing Texas Fetal Pain Legislation"—and this comes from District Eleven of that particular organization. "The Texas District of the American Congress of Obstetricians and Gynecologists, Texas ACOG, opposes HB 16 by Representative Laubenberg. Texas ACOG opposes HB 16 and other legislative proposals that are not based on sound science or that attempt to prescribe how physicians should care for their individual patients. As a district of the nation's leading authority on women's health, our role is to ensure that policy proposals accurately reflect the best available medical knowledge.

Terminology: The use of appropriate standard terminology is essential. A child is a person from birth until the age of legal majority. The proper term for the second to eighth week is embryo. The embryo becomes a fetus at ten weeks. The term fetus is the correct term to use until birth. The language regarding post-fertilization age is rarely used outside in vitro fertilization. The post-fertilization age of the embryo or fetus is not known. There is inherent variability in the timing of ovulation, fertilization, and implantation. Obstetricians, gynecologists, and the medical community at large use the first day of the last menstrual period, L.M.P., to date pregnancies. Post-fertilization dating is not an accurate substitute and should not be referenced in legislation.

Fetal Pain: The statement quotes: "Substantial medical evidence recognizes that an unborn child is capable of experiencing pain by not later than 20 weeks after fertilization" end quote, is not accurate. And of course members we know that quote was in the bill analysis as well as in the bill itself. The medical profession produced a rigorous scientific review of the available evidence on fetal pain in the Journal of the American Medical Association, JAMA, in 2005. Pain perception requires conscious recognition or awareness of a noxious stimulus. Neither withdrawal reflexes, nor hormonal stress responses to invasive procedures prove the existence of fetal pain, because they can be elicited by non-painful stimuli and occur without conscious cortical processing. Fetal awareness of noxious stimuli requires functional, thalamacortical connections. Thalamacortical fibers begin appearing between 23 to 30 weeks gestational age, which electroencephalography suggests the capacity for functional pain perception in pre-term neonates probably does not exist before 29 or 30 weeks. The review concluded that fetal perception of pain is unlikely before the third trimester; more recent studies confirm that finding. The Royal College of Obstetricians and Gynecologists, ARCOG, is the UK-based equivalent to ACOG, with 12,500 members worldwide, and representation in over 100 countries on all 6 continents. In 2010, ARCOG rigorously reviewed the scientific literature and, quote, "In reviewing the neuro anatomical and physiological evidence of the fetus, it was apparent the connections from the periphery to the cortex are not intact before 24 weeks of gestation and, as most neuroscientists believe that the cortex is un—is necessary for pain perception, it can be concluded that the fetus cannot experience pain in any sense prior to this gestation." End quote. Supporters of fetal pain legislation only present studies which support the claim of fetal pain prior to third trimester. When weighed together with other available information including the JAMA and ARCOG studies, supporter's conclusions do not stand.

Fetal Viability: Most obstetrician gynecologists understand fetal viability as occurring near 24 weeks gestation, utilizing L.M.P. dating. Supporters of fetal pain present misleading evidence about fetal viability, especially in using post-fertilization age instead of L.M.P. dating—falsely implying high survey-survival rates among neonates that are overwhelmingly pre-viable. Supporters may point to the survival of live born infants in a June, 2009 JAMA's study, but fail to mention the vast majority of infants born prior to 24 completed weeks L.M.P. died prior to or during birth. In this study 93 percent of infants at 22 weeks died, 66 percent at 23 weeks, and 40 percent at 24 weeks. Ninety-one percent of those that lived were admitted to the N.I.C.U. Also not mentioned by supporters is the fact that survival alone is not the only end-point for neonatologists. Intact survival is; in this same study 98 percent of infants born at 22 weeks L.M.P. and 91 percent born at 23 weeks L.M.P. had at least one major medical problem, such as hemorrhaging brain or a bowel. The American Academy of Pediatrics Committee on Fetus and Newborns, states that the incidence of moderate or severe neuro developmental disability in surviving children assessed at the age of 18 to 30 months is high, approximately 30 to 50 percent, and remains at that high level until 25 weeks L.M.P. Babies delivered at these gestational ages, often suffer hemorrhaging bowel, blindness, deafness and stroke as a result of their premature delivery.

Fetal Anomalies: Many fetal anomalies can be diagnosed before

20 weeks. Others are not diagnosed until around 20 weeks. HB 16 provides an inadequate exception for severe fetal abnormalities. This exception puts into statute how a doctor should exercise medical judgment and interferes with the private nature of deciding what to do when a fetus has been diagnosed with severe fetal abnormalities. There are numerous fetal anomalies that are regularly detected only after 20 weeks. While chromosomal anomalies can generally be diagnosed by 20 weeks, some low-risk couples do not elect to have testing and instead learn that their fetus has a chromosomal ano—anomaly during routine ultrasound later in pregnancy, an ultrasound that is often performed at 18 to 20 weeks gestational age. Moreover, many lethal or serious fetal problems that are not compatible with life outside of the womb are caused by conditions that are structural, not chromosomal, and are not susceptible to testing by amniocentesis. These can only be diagnosed by detailed ultrasound examinations. Many tests cannot definitively diagnose grave conditions affecting a pregnancy prior to 20 weeks because the fetus is not sufficiently developed for those conditions to be detected, even in cases where an ultrasound detects indications of a structural anomaly prior to 20 weeks. Additional tests, such as amniocentesis or echocardiogram, are often necessary to confirm the diagnosis. Scheduling those additional tests and obtaining the results will take additional time, often up to 2 weeks. By the time a diagnosis is confirmed by a specialist capable of diagnosing these anomalies, the pregnancy has often progressed beyond 20 weeks. As a result, a woman whose fetus is critically impaired often will not learn about that fact until well into the second trimester. The medical difficulty if not impossibility of diagnosing many of these lethal, structural defects before 20 weeks, is heightened by the fact that additional tests and doctor's appointments are often needed to confirm the anomaly as discussed above. Once the diagnosis is confirmed, many couples need additional time to make a well-informed, careful decision about whether to terminate a wanted pregnancy. General obstetricians who suspect a problem based on an ultrasound at 18 to 20 weeks often refer their patient to a perinatologist,

the relevant specialist for confirmatory study and then diagnosis. These confirmatory tests take additional time, sometimes several weeks to schedule and obtain results, particularly for women who live in rural or underserved areas. The final diagnosis will thus regularly take place near or after 20 weeks.

Life of the mother: HB 16 provides a limited exception for the life and health of the mother. However, it fails to entirely protect women for whom pregnancy poses serious health risks. Under the exception in HB 16 a physician can perform a termination only once a medical condition has so compromised the woman's health that she requires a quote, "immediate abortion" end quote. In order to, quote, "avert her death or a serious risk of substantial and irreversible physical impairment of a major bodily function" end quote. By requiring doctors to wait until a woman faces immediate injury or death it indefensibly jeopardizes a patient's health. ACOG opposes HB 16 and strongly urges the legislature to closely examine and follow scientific facts and medical evidence in its consideration of this and other healthcare legislation. We stand ready to provide you with factual information on medical issues that come before the legislature and hope you will contact us at anytime." And it's signed, "respectfully, Lisa M. Hollier, M.D.M.P.H., SACOG, Chair of the Texas District of the American Congress of Obstetricians and Gynecologists."

Another statement by ACOG opposing SB 5, by Senator Hager, and HB 60, by Representative Laubenberg:

"Texas ACOG opposes SB 5 by Senator Hager and HB 60 by Representative Laubenberg. SB 5, HB 60, is an accumulation of all the measures we opposed during the 83rd regular session and remain opposed to in this special session. The Texas District of the American Congress of Obstetricians and Gynecologists, ACOG, opposes SB 5, HB 60 and other legislative proposals that are not based on sound science or that attempt to prescribe how physicians should care for the individual patients. As a district of the nation's leading authority and women's health our role is to ensure that policy proposals accurately reflect the best available medical knowledge. SB 5, HB 60 will not enhance patient safety or improve the quality of care that women receive. This bill does not promote women's health, but erodes it by denying women in Texas the benefits of well researched, safe, and proven protocols. Texas ACOG opposes 20-week ban/fetal pain provisions.

Terminology: The use of appropriate standard terminology is essential. Embryo is the proper term to use for the second to eighth week of pregnancy. Fetus is the correct term to use until birth. Post-fertilization is rarely used outside of in vitro fertilization. The medical community uses the first day of the last menstrual period, L.M.P. to date pregnancies. Post-fertilization is not an accurate substitute.

Fetal Pain: No credible scientific evidence exists of fetal pain perception pre-viability. The medical profession produced a rigorous scientific review of evidence on fetal pain in the Journal of American Medical Association, JAMA, in 2005. Fetal perception of pain is not confirmed prior to the third trimester. Perception of pain is only confirmed after viability. Most obstetricians . . . excuse me, there was another heading . . .

Fetal Viability: Most obstetrician gynecologists understand fetal viability as occurring near 24 weeks gestation utilizing L.M.P. dating. Supporters of fetal pain present misleading evidence about fetal viability, especially in using post fertilization age instead of L.M.P. dating, and falsely implying high survival rates among neonates. They're overwhelmingly pre-viable.

Fetal Anomalies: Many fetal anomalies can be diagnosed before 20 weeks; others are not diagnosed until around 20 weeks. The committee substitute for Senate Bill 5 provides an inadequate exception for severe fetal abnormalities. This exception puts into statute how a doctor should exercise medical judgment and interferes with the private nature of deciding what to do when a fetus has been diagnosed with a severe fetal abnormality.

Life of the mother: SB 5, HB 60 fails to entirely protect women for whom pregnancy poses serious health risks. By requiring doctors to wait until a woman faces immediate injury or death, It indefensively jeopardizes a patient's health. Instead doctors are forced to compromise patient health by waiting until a woman's condition deteriorates and becomes life-threatening or severely debilitating. Texas ACOG opposes provisions that treat women as if they cannot make their own medical decision. Committee substitute for Senate Bill 5 would require a woman to come to an ambulatory surgical center, A.S.C., to take a pill for a medical abortion. She would then have to return a second time to the A.S.C. to be watched taking the second pill within the next 24 to 48 hours. Requiring a woman to physically come in to take a second dose increases the risk of her not being able to return. This increases the chance for hemorrhages, blood transfusion, and emergent D and C. Women outside of Dallas, Houston, San Antonio, and Austin will have to travel long distances to find a clinic that meets A.S.C. regulations. These burdensome requirements will make these services harder to access, as well as make these services more costly. Texas ACOG opposes provisions dictating protocol for physicians to follow when prescribing certain drugs. SB 5, HB 60 weakens standards of care and patient safety. SB 5, HB 60 requires providers to follow a protocol that has been proven to be less effective, more costly, and causes more detrimental side effects for women than care that is currently available and widely used. Committee substitute for Senate Bill 5 has permissive language allowing dosage amounts that follow the ACOG practice bulletin guidelines as they existed on January 1st, 2013. However, this is still codifying standard of care, and is dangerous in the long term. Science and medicine evolve quicker than our laws. SB 5, HB 60 physicians can be—under SB 5, HB 60, physicians can be punished for striving to provide the highest quality of care for their patients—the women of Texas. SB 5, HB 60 threatens the doctor-patient relationship. SB 5, HB 60 places an unacceptable level of control over the doctor-patient relationship in the hands of the legislature, essentially allowing the legislature to practice medicine. SB 5, HB 60 creates medical protocol for physicians, dictates what to document, what tests to perform, what medications to prescribe, and when to schedule follow-up appointments. SB 5, HB 60 interferes with a doctor's ability to use his or her professional judgment to determine the appropriate medical care in each individual patient's unique circumstance. It undermines the standard of care and restricts the ability of physicians to prescribe and direct medication use. SB 5, HB 60 interferes with physician's ability to establish an individual care plan. Texas ACOG opposes overreaching requirements for abortion facilities. SB 5, HB 60 requires additional standards that are unnecessary and unsupported by scientific evidence. SB 5, HB 60 does not promote the public health objective it claims to enhance. In fact, it harms public health by restricting access to safe, legal and accessible abortion services. Late term abortions, 16 weeks and later, are already required to be provided at a facility licensed as an ambulatory surgical center. SB 5, HB 60 has unintended consequences that make the treatment of certain conditions, for example, ectopic pregnancies, more difficult and expensive. Ectopic pregnancies are frequently treated in outpatient facilities and physician office settings. SB 5, HB 60 may prevent doctors from treating cases as they normally would. Ectopic pregnancies must be reported to D.S.H.S. as emergency abortions. This could result in physicians losing exemption from abortion facility licensing requirements. Positive patient outcomes will decrease. Medical costs will increase. It also affects more providers and facilities than just Planned Parenthood or traditional abortion facilities. Texas ACOG opposes unnecessary requirements that may be extremely difficult and in some cases impossible to meet without a basis in public health or safety. SB 5, HB 60 requires hospital-admitting privileges for physicians performing an outpatient procedure that bares low risk. No other outpatient procedure requires a physician to have active admitting privileges in a hospital within a specific distance. Requirements for admitting privileges vary from hospital to hospital. Some hospitals bar physicians that perform termination from being awarded hospital privileges. Processes for approval . . . "

Thank you Mr. President. "Processes for approval of admitting privileges can take a lengthy amount of time, sometimes as long as licensure and board certification. A physician may have active admitting privileges but not within a 30-mile radius. This is especially problematic for rural areas where hospitals are scarce. Not all hospitals may meet the requirement of providing obstetrical or gynecological healthcare service. There is not a special designation for hospitals providing OB/GYN services. This provision is vague and could have extensive consequences. Criminally penalizing physicians for performing a legal procedure is inappropriate and prevents physicians from performing a legal procedure is inappropriate, criminally penalizing physicians for performing a legal procedure is inappropriate and prevents physicians from exercising medical judgment in order to treat their patients as they see fit. ACOG opposes SB 5, HB 60 and strongly urges the legislature to closely examine and follow scientific facts and medical evidence in its consideration of this and other healthcare legislation. We stand ready to provide you with factual information on medical issues that come before the legislature and hope you will contact us at anytime." And it is signed, "respectfully, Lisa M. Hollier, M.D. S.M.P.H. SACOG, Chair Texas District American Congress of the Obstetricians and Gynecologists."

And then this letter from ACOG related to admitting privileges, which was the bill filed by Senator Taylor.

"Texas ACOG opposes SB 1198, by Senator Taylor." It's dated April 16th, 2013.

"Dear Chair Nelson and members of the Senate Health and Human Services Committee: Thank you for the opportunity to present this written—written testimony in opposition to SB 1198. The Texas district of the American Congress of Obstetricians and Gynecologists represents more than 3600 physicians and partners in women's health. Texas ACOG opposes SB 1198 by Senator Taylor. While ACOG recognizes that the issue of support for or opposition to abortion is a personal matter and respects the need and responsibility of its members to determine their individual positions, as an organization, ACOG recognizes that abortion is an essential healthcare service and opposes laws regulating medical care that are unsupported by scientific evidence and that are not necessary to achieve an important public health objective. SB 1198 sets up unnecessary requirements that may be extremely difficult and in some cases impossible to meet without a basis in public health or safety. Requirements for admitting privileges vary from hospital to hospital. The process for approval of admitting privileges can take a lengthy amount of time, sometimes as long as licensure and board certification. We are not aware of other outpatient procedures that require a physician to have active admitting privileges in a hospital within a certain distance. A physician may have active admitting privileges, but not within a 30-mile radius. This is especially problematic for rural areas where hospitals are scarce. Not all hospitals may meet the requirement of providing obstetrical or gynecological healthcare service. There is not a special designation for hospitals providing OB/GYN services. This provision is vague and could have extensive consequences. Creating unnecessary requirements and criminalizing—criminally penalizing physicians for performing a legal procedure is inappropriate and prevents physicians from exercising their medical judgment in order to treat their patients as they see fit. For the reasons outlined above, Texas ACOG opposes SB 1198." It's signed "respectfully, Lisa M. Hollier M.D.M.P.H., SACOG, Chair of the Texas District of the American Congress of Obstetricians and Gynecologists."

A letter again from ACOG, this time opposing SB 18, by Senator Patrick.

"ACOG opposes SB 18 by Senator Patrick" and it's dated, June 12th, 2013: "The Texas District of the American Congress of Obstetricians and Gynecologists, ACOG, represents more than 3,600 physicians and partners in women's health. ACOG opposes Senate Bill 18 because it is a significant intrusion into the doctor-patient relationship, legislating the practice of medicine. This bill unfortunately illustrates the perils of attempting to legislate a particular protocol, increases expenses, and undermines the quality of care for women. First, this bill would require physicians to practice medicine that is not evidence based. Since the F.D.A. approval of the regimen in this legislation in 2000, additional clinical studies have identified improvements in the treatment of medical abortion. The American College of Obstetricians and Gynecologists makes the following statement in practice bulletin number 67, entitled, 'Medical Management of Abortion': 'compared to the F.D.A. approved regimen, mifepristone or misoprostol regimens using 200 milligrams of mifepristone or misoprostol, orally and 800 M.C.G., of misoprostol vaginally are associated with a decreased rate of continuing pregnancies, decreased time to expulsion, fewer side effects, improved complete abortion rates, lower costs for women, with pregnancies up to 16 . . . 63 days of gestation based on L.M.P., the last missed period.' The F.D.A. approved regimen, which this bill would mandate, that physicians prescribe for their patients, requires a 600 milligram dose of mifepristone, which is three times greater than in the non-F.D.A. approved evidence based regimen, that ACOG endorses above. Furthermore, the misoprostol dose, a lower dose on face value is given orally by the F.D.A. approved regimen, whereas, it is administered vaginally in the evidence based regimen. Oral administration results in higher peak levels of the drug in the blood stream, which in turn results in greater side effects for women. Vaginal administration not only decreases side effects, but also results in greater uterine contractility. Together, as in the evidence based regimen, a lower dose of mifepristone combined with a vaginal dose of misoprostol, acts superiorly to the F.D.A. approved regimen. Multiple randomized controlled trials, which are considered the gold standard of experimental design for research studies, have consistently demonstrated that the F.D.A. approved regimen is associated with greater side effects in women, roughly three times higher costs and lower overall success rates: 92 percent compared to 95 to 99 percent success with the evidence based regimen. The F.D.A. approved protocol for these medications is no safer than the evidence based protocols recommended by the American College of Obstetricians and Gynecologists,

The Royal College of Obstetricians and Gynecologists, and the World Health Organization. This legislation prohibits, in fact creates penalties for the act of prescribing a medication regimen that has in the simplest of terms, simply been proven to be far superior to the F.D.A. approved regimen. Under this legislation physicians would face penalties for striving to provide the highest quality of care for the women of Texas. Second, SB 18 places an unacceptable level of control over the doctor-patient setting in the hands of the legislature, essentially allowing the legislature to practice medicine. Again, this bill actually creates a medical protocol for physicians, dictating what medications to prescribe, what doses to use, what to document, questions to ask the patient, and when to schedule follow-up appointments. For example, the bill requires that patients be scheduled to return to the physician that prescribes the medication for a follow-up visit within a specific 14-day time frame written into the law. I absolutely agree that women should have a follow-up exam to ensure a successful termination with no complications. However, frequently this follow-up care is better and more conveniently provided by a primary care provider or referring physician in their own community, particularly for women in remote areas who may have to travel long distances to access specialized gynecologic services. There is a medical necessity for follow-up care, but no medical rational that this follow-up care must be provided by the prescribing physician. This requirement can create a distance and access barrier for patients with no medical rationale or benefits. Third, SB 18 interferes with a doctor's ability to use his or her professional judgment to determine the appropriate medical care in each individual patient's unique circumstances. Patients have spent years acquiring the specialized knowledge . . . " excuse me "physicians have spent years acquiring the specialized knowledge, skills, clinical and research training needed to individualize a plan of care for their patients, based upon their unique medical and surgical family and social histories. It is critically important that physicians have a toolbox, so to speak, to pull from when designing a plan of care for a patient, because we rarely find that one size fits all. For this reason, particularly in the setting of prescribing medication, it is standard medical practice in the United States for physicians to prescribe F.D.A. approved medicines in doses or contacts that were not specifically approved by the F.D.A., so long as the alternative use is supported by adequate research. These are sometimes referred to as off-label for evidence-based uses. Every physician has prescribed drugs for off-label uses, perhaps to your wives, daughters, sisters, or mothers: birth control pills for endometriosis, misoprostol for labor induction, magnesium sulfate to reduce the chance of neurologic complications for pre-term newborns. These are all considered off-label uses standardly employed based on available evidence. Finally, legislation of a single specific medical protocol prevents an opportunity for continuous quality improvement. One of the pillars of medicine is the ability to compare protocols and advance the quality of the medical care that is provided. If this bill were to become law, we would be unable to test potentially better treatments and would need to wait for a legislative session to change the law to implement improvement in care that has developed elsewhere. The bill will not enhance public safety. This bill will not improve the quality of care that women receive. This bill does not promote women's health. SB 18 would deny women in Texas the benefits of well-researched, safe, and proven protocols that currently exist." And it's signed, "respectfully, Lisa M. Hollier, M.D.M.P.H., SACOG, Chair of the Texas District, American Congress of Obstetricians and Gynecologists."

Now members, I am going to begin to read testimony from people who were unable to testify before the house committee. These were people who came to the capitol and waited many, many, many, hours for the chance for their voices to be heard. And unfortunately the chair of the committee hearing testimony, at one point, around 1 am, made a decision that no longer would testimony be accepted. In his words, "because it had become repetitive." An answer to that was provided very poignantly by a young woman who was there to testify, apologizing that the chair believed her testimony on such an important issue was repetitive, when for her it was her individual story, and she felt, her individual right to speak on the impacts of legislation like this. Because that testimony was not allowed, I thought it particularly appropriate today to use the opportunity with this microphone in my hand to give voice to the people who were not able to provide their voices as part of that testimony. Because that is truly what we are to be: representatives, senators, who are elected to serve our communities and to give voice to them on this senate floor. Below are 31 testimonies that I have received from people who had registered to offer testimony at Thursday's State Affairs Committee Meeting, but were denied the opportunity to do so.

Regarding House Bill 60 and House Bill 16, offered by State Representative, Jody Laubenberg, June 20th, 2013. From Amy, I'm sorry, Amy if I mispronounce your name, Arynbide, or Arynbeady.

"House District 121 Representative Strauss. Thank you Chair Strauss and Committee for allowing me to testify," she was going to begin "I live in House District 121 and I am a constituent of Chair Strauss. My name is Amy Arynbide and my Father, Dr. George Arynbide, or Arynbied, was an abortion provider. He was born in Chicago to a single, Mexican immigrant woman, who worked three jobs at a cannery during the depression to provide for her three children. My father put himself through college and then medical school and started off his career as an anesthesiologist. After a 20-year career as an anesthesiologist, he went through residency again, and became an OB/GYN in the early '70's. In addition to a full time OB/GYN practice, he began performing abortions in the mid '70's, shortly after *Roe v. Wade* in San Antonio and traveled once a week to provide reproductive healthcare at a clinic in Laredo. Growing up, I knew my father was a doctor and delivered babies, but I didn't understand the extent of his profession until one day when I was in the fifth grade. A fellow student and her parents told me that my father kills babies and I was aghast. I knew he delivered babies, he delivered me, but I didn't understand what they were talking about. I went home and confronted my parents, at which time they explained to me what an abortion was. I didn't understand. My father explained that while keeping a baby or putting up a baby for adoption were options many girls and women chose— were options that many chose, sometimes that was not truly an option. Many of his patients were really young or didn't have the means to provide for a child and that being pregnant could end many of the opportunities that could better a woman's life, like getting an education. I still didn't really understand, so my father decided to take me to the clinic, to Laredo, to give me an idea of the women that he helped each week. We drove through an impoverished town that I could hardly believe was in the United States that I grew up in. The waiting room was filled with women and girls from all over South Texas, girls that had no other options for reproductive healthcare, except this one clinic for hundreds of miles. The girls were as young as I was, around twelve, and I could tell that they did not grow up with any means. After this trip to Laredo I realized that my father was a hero. He helped women and girls that had nowhere else to go and who didn't have many options. He provided care, health services, and an option that could make their life better. The first year I lived in Austin, I got harassing phone calls from a gentleman looking for Dr. Arynbide's son. When my roommate told him that Dr. Arynbide's daughter lived there and not his son, he demanded to speak to me. He said that he worked with my father and owed him money. He wanted his home address so that he could send the check. When I told him that my father had worked at the same address for 20 years and he could send it there, and when I asked him for his contact information, he refused. That's when I realized just how dangerous my father's job really was. Contrary to what some witnesses may say, the doctors who provide abortions are heroes and you cannot do this work unless you truly believe in women. My father wore a Kevlar vest to work every day, had an FBI agent assigned to us, and chose houses in gated communities because he received threats from the violent opposition every day. In order to work one day a week in Laredo, he paid more in malpractice insurance than the money that he made there. My father was a hero.

He believed that every woman deserved a chance to make her life better. He believed in access to education and choices that would facilitate that. My father provided comprehensive sex education and knowledge and choices for me that allowed me to go to college, go to law school, and plan my family when I was ready. Because of his influence and what he did for women, I have two beautiful boys that I am ready to raise in a world that I strive to make a better place."

This next testimony is from Nancy Cardanyez, from Austin, Texas.

"As a woman, I have struggled to understand how something as personal as my body is constantly a part of the political battleground. Furthermore, as a woman from South Texas, I am appalled that abortion clinics in the valley that provide excellent and safe healthcare will no longer be available. Women seeking safe abortions will have to drive hundreds of miles for the healthcare they deserve. Senator Bob Deuell called clinics, quote, 'money centers,' end quote. The purpose of these centers is not to make money, but to give women access to excellent healthcare and safe abortions. These centers cannot afford an extra $40,000 per month. Imposing these regulations will not only shut down 37 clinics, but leave women who do not live in Dallas, San Antonio, and Houston to fend for themselves. Why don't we look at this bill for what it really is? A political maneuver that strips away the right of a woman to choose what to do with her own body and puts it in the hands of men who are more interested in fulfilling a religious, political agenda. What this bill does is disenfranchises certain sectors of the state, like El Paso, and actively discriminates against rural areas of Texas. Why don't you actually sit down and talk with your female constituents? We are voters. We have a voice and we are responsible enough to make decisions over our own bodies. This bill strips the basic right of a woman to control her own body through one of the most difficult decisions of her life. House Bill 60 takes this decision out of the hands of a woman, her family, and her doctor, as it neglects the complexities of reality. I ask you to oppose HB 60. Thank you for your time.

This testimony from Samantha Fredrickson of Austin, House District 48, Donna Howard.

"My name is Samantha Frederickson; I am a woman, a Texas voter, and representative Donna Howard's District 48, an attorney and a person of faith. I'm speaking on behalf of myself. I strongly urge you to oppose HB 16 and HB 60. The legislature has no business regulating what I choose to do with my own body. I am very lucky in that I have not had to seek an abortion. I am also very lucky that I live in a country where abortions are safe and legal, should I have to make the difficult and painful decision to ever have one. Please don't take that choice away from me. If I, or any other woman out there, needs to seek an abortion for whatever very personal reasons, I would like to know that it is a possibility. These bills would make it nearly impossible for women in this state to seek a safe, legal abortion, for whatever reason they choose to. I am new to Texas and I've lived in lots of different states. Before moving here I was never very concerned about women's equality because I felt that the law respected me and treated me as fully equal. I thought, 'Oh, times are not like they were in my parents and grandparents days. Women truly do have equality now so why should I be worried about it?' But frankly, since moving to Texas, my opinion on the matter has drastically changed. The law in Texas treats me as though I am a second-class citizen. I love Texas. It's a great place to live and I hope to stay here, but I do not appreciate that my legislators do not respect me or treat me as an equal citizen. After everything that generations before me fought for, it is incredibly unfortunate that I live in a state where none of that seems to matter to the lawmakers. Please end this war on women and do not pass these bills. They will do nothing to protect women and are not crafted with women's healthcare in mind. A woman's right to access family planning services is vital to her ability to succeed in life and in her career. But severely limiting a woman's ability to choose when and how she will have a family, the legislature is curtailing women's possibilities, and the message this legislature is sending with these bills is that a woman's role is solely to have children. Whether or not I, or any other woman, chooses to have children is a choice that only we can make. The legislature needs to stay out of this decision. Please stand up for women's equality and reject these bills. Women are smart. We are smart enough to be able to make a decision about how to plan a family without the legislature interfering. And as lawmakers, the women of Texas are looking to you to ensure that our rights and interests are protected. Please do your job and reject this legislation, which is detrimental to the health and security of all women in Texas. Thank you."

This next testimony, from Gary L. Oldham, from Roundrock, House District 52, Representative Larry Gonzalez district.

"Thank you Chair and Committee for allowing me to testify. My name is Gary Oldham and I am a constituent of Representative Larry Gonzalez and I'm here to testify an opposition to HB 16 because I am immensely concerned about women's health along with children's health, and men's health, and a rejection of science by this body. I have heard much rhetoric that cavalierly rejects the concept of gun safety legislation that uses the illogical argument that criminals and those who want to get guns, and can't do so legally, will continue to do so. If true, the unconstitutional banning of legal abortion by making safe, legal, abortion inaccessible to a vast number of Texas women will not cause it to cease. It will just make it illegal and vastly more dangerous. Science is being routinely rejected by this body as well as by the state board of education. The wonderful thing about science is that it's true whether you believe in it or not. Science is not dependent on your belief or mine. It simply is. To reject the collective science and medical wisdom of the American Medical Association, the Centers for Disease Control, and the American College of Obstetricians and Gynecologists is embarrassing folly. Calling it speculation is an embarrassment to any sentient being. Calling these peer-reviewed findings by the best and brightest of our medical community 'speculations' is the most transparent desperate political maneuvering. Calling science speculative, while supporting one's argument with unverified anecdotal stories would not pass muster in third grade. Once upon a time, mankind believed that the sun revolved around the earth. The church officially believed it. World leaders believed it. The man and woman on the street believed it. Scientists who claimed otherwise became outcasts, were ex-communicated, were put on trial for their blasphemy. But none of those rejections, by the arrogantly ignorant, changed the facts. Rejecting objective facts and science, because they conflict with our ideology, is the greatest form of ignorance imaginable. Promoting ideologies that conflict with facts, forcing our ideology upon others, and then causing irreparable harm to others is inexcusable and unforgivable. Vote no on HB 16 and protect women's health and rights. HB 16, like HB 60, is merely another effort by the American Legislative Research Council (ALRC) and their state representative to voice legislation that is bad for your average human being, your average constituent, and that benefits corporations and corporate interests. If you are genuinely interested in the health and wellbeing of Texas women, you will not implement further draconian legislation to make even worse the already onerous restrictions of Texas women. Do the right thing and vote no on HB 16. Thank you."

This from Katherine Kennemer-Gennett, Austin, Texas.

"I attended the hearing on Thursday evening, for HB 60 and HB 16 and registered to give my testimony. I was unable to give my testimony before the chairman ended the committee meeting. My name is Kelly Gennett. I'm speaking on my own behalf. I'm represented in the Texas house by Elliot Naishtat. I'm here to testify against HB 60 and HB 16. It was very easy for me to be here tonight, I live about one and a half miles from the capital, so I'd like to speak in honor of women who live far away from Austin or who did not have the financial means to be here tonight. There are 5.7 million women in Texas between the ages of 15 and 54—the child-bearing years. With 700 of us here, we each represent over 8,000 women, 8,000 women with unique stories. I'm humbled by the stories of the women and men in this room—people who have had pasts so different than mine. Going forward, we 700 Texans, each representing 8,000 more, will continue to have unique lives. We all have the right to exercise our reproductive freedom, and Mr. Chairman and members of the house, you do not know what it is right for me, for them, for our families, or for our health. I've been a patient of my OB/GYN's since 2000. He and I have worked through a pregnancy and birth of one of my three children. He knows my medical history and has helped me to choose my birth control. I am a grown woman, who after having born three children, knows the very real, emotional, financial, and spiritual weight of having that experience. It is hard, quite expensive and scary at times, and it is intensely personal. You are cordially not invited to share that experience with me. I am a grown woman, a voter, a citizen and a U.S constitutionally protected American. You are cordially not invited to treat me as though I am not. You are trying to pass a law to appease voters that make up a tiny sliver of our state's population; the most conservative branch of a conservative party. That is why you have committee meetings on short notice and shut down citizen comments and have follow-up meetings in tiny rooms with no cameras. It is why you didn't attempt to pass these laws abridging the constitutional rights affirmed in Roe v. Wade during the regular session. Lieutenant Governor Dewhurst and Governor Perry have suspended the voting rules during the special session because that is the only way you can pass this legislation. Polls show the majority of Texans do not support you. You game the system politically and use all the tricks because the majority of Americans and Texans and women would not approve of what you are doing. Meanwhile, the 700 here, representing the 5.7 million others are shining a light on your actions. We will not sit down while you attempt to strip us of our self determination. We will not be quiet while you pander to the particular views of a minority of Texans who do not want us to make our own decisions and who continually punish poor women for wanting to have control over their reproductive lives. You are going to kill women, moms, sisters, daughters and friends who will be disenfranchised from safe, available medical care in rural Texas. I came here to champion the rights of all women, of all families, of all economic means, and living in all parts of our very vast state to have what I have: the right to make medical decisions about their reproductive lives. I came here for the birth control but I am staying here for the fight."

From Julie Gillis, of Austin, Texas:

"Hi, my name is Julie Gillis and I am an Austin resident and a Texas native. Donna Dukes is my representative and Kirk Watson is my senator. My mother was born in 1928 and her childhood was marked by the Great Depression, World War II, and F.D.R.'s policies that helped America come back from economic devastation. She also witnessed massive social change in the '60's social justice movement; she was adamantly for, but also the pill. Prior to the pill, people did indeed have sex, lots of it. To hear her tell it, back then, unmarried women couldn't get the pill on their own and even married women had to get clearance from the husband so her doctor could prescribe it. She was overjoyed at the pill and abortion rights because she recognized that women's body's belonged to them and access to reproductive services meant freedom. She had Alzheimer's the last ten years and so she's been shielded from the backlash on women. She'd have been horrified to see the chipping away of Planned Parenthood, sex education in the schools, and the influence of the religious right on reproductive rights. She'd also have tied that chipping away directly to the desire to have a permanent poverty class, a kind of economic slavery class and destruction of our economic safety. She'd have been ashamed of our elected officials for allowing this to happen. Hell, for encouraging it. She would have said that people who are poor and kept from education wind up being desperate. They take bad jobs because that's all there is. They find themselves trapped in marriages or pregnancies. The poverty class keeps itself locked in because there aren't policies in place to help. That being said, she, like me, would probably want to see abortion rates drop. Abstinence only doesn't work because we've got 11 billion people on the planet. People like sex. Sex is a good thing. It's such a good thing that I helped produce a storytelling series about it, smart, funny, risky, stories about the human condition and sexuality. If you want to reduce abortion take my advice and follow these three steps: 1) Teach everyone about how their bodies work. Comprehensive, age appropriate sex ed is a moral issue and a human right. Education is power. Don't deny people education. 2) Offer many varieties of easily accessible, low-cost birth control options. Don't chip away at Planned Parenthood. Make sure there are even more. Access is power. Don't deny people access. Make sure a social . . . .3) Make sure a social safety net is in place filled with unions, workers rights, fair wages, fair and ethical bank practices, health services, state funded daycare services, insurance and more. Those finding themselves pregnant who want to proceed with the pregnancy have resources. Resources are power. Don't deny people resources. I fully expect all of those points to be rebuffed with anti-choice tropes about loving babies and loving women. What a strange kind of love. A strange love to refuse to teach people about sex and put myths of purity on young girls. A strange love to force women to keep babies inside them that are wanted but dying and causing trauma for the mother. A strange love to ask rape victims to have a vaginal probe inserted inside them against their will; that's not love, that's sickness. But then it's not about love, is it? It's about economics and a perpetual poverty class and about keeping power from those that have the right to it. Do the right thing for Texas women. We won't back down."

From Nicole Goadd, Austin, Texas:

"There's a popular bumper sticker that says, 'I'm not from Texas but I got here as fast as I could.' That's me, coming from rural Louisiana; I've always heard how great Texas is. And now that I'm here, I feel as if it's a place in which I could truly blossom. Our economy is strong. Our unemployment is lower than national averages and even our housing market is up. We're so wonderful that our own governor feels compelled to recruit folks from California and New York to move to our state to create better lives for themselves. It's an exciting time to be a Texan if you're here for business. But if you are here as a woman, who is concerned about her most deserved and protected rights, you might want to reconsider your trek down to the Lonestar state. This state has made a travesty of its handling of a woman's right to contraceptive advice, education, and safe medically approved methods of abortion. We are being told that we no longer have the opportunity to make our own choices; to access healthcare wherever we may reside, and that the laws our federal government guarantees us do not count here in the state of Texas. Lord knows I love to brag about our breakfast tacos but aren't we more than good food, great business, and wide open spaces? We should be champions of a fantastic quality of life for all Texans, whether they be aggies or longhorns, natives, or transplants, men or women, or rich or poor. I want to know that the state who holds itself up so high, they want to take on the east and west coast, will protect and defend my rights to female health-care. I know we can be a 21st century top of the line state who attracts the best and brightest talent. But we need to make sure that across the board; we live in the 21st century and ensure that all Texans will be treated equally. I ask you to think about the Texas you want to live in. It's going to be great but we've got to strike down this bill to get that."

This from Andrea Grimes, Austin, Texas:

"My name is Andrea Grimes and I'm here representing myself testifying in strong opposition to HB 60. I am one of Representative Naishtat constituents here in Austin. I believe that practical effects of this bill are clear. It would significantly reduce access to safe, legal abortion in the state of Texas and that scares me and I'm a Texan lady so not a lot scares me. I've done some barrel racing. I've seem big old snakes out in the hill country and bar brawls on 6th street. But this legislation is terrifying and I'll tell you why. The so-called pre-born pain act ignores sound mainstream medical science supported by The American Medical Association and The American College of Obstetricians and Gynecologists. The restrictions are on the administration of medical abortions would prevent Texans in rural areas from safely and swiftly obtaining medication that would allow them to end their pregnancies without multiple unnecessary visits to a doctor's office or if this legislation passes an ambulatory surgical center hundreds of miles from home. And I've yet to hear from a legislator who can provide any evidence whatsoever that shows abortions performed in ambulatory surgical centers are safer than those performed in licensed abortion facilities. There is a reason you're hearing from me and women who look and sound like me today. I am an affluent, white, English speaking woman with a flexible job, who lives in an urban area. I will always be able to get an abortion if I need one. But the Texans who will be disproportionately negatively affected by this legislation are not able to take time off work, arrange childcare, and drive hundreds of miles to sit in a cold, sterile room, either in hopes of getting an abortion or in hopes of testifying at a capitol committee hearing. But in closing, what scares me most of all, is the confusing and appalling fact that some of the members of this committee are viewed earlier today that intent is not important when drafting this legislation. If that is the case, I wonder why these bills include language about a compelling state interest in fetal pain in the first place. If we are legislating without intent we are shooting blind and as a Texas lady, I know one of the things we're real proud of here, is our aim. I would like to respectfully ask that you vote to keep state government out of my uterus."

And this from Shelly Hyem, from Austin, Texas:

"My name is Shelly Hyem and I'm representing myself and my opposition of HB 60. As a young teenager, my political and religious beliefs were that of my parents, which is to say prolife. I was raised in Texas and went through our public school sex education system. I was taught abstinence. So was a good friend of mine, at age 14, came to me frightened she was pregnant and she saw abortion as her only option. I was conflicted. I urged her to consider other options. She looked at me and explained that she was going to do it no matter what. It didn't matter if she didn't have the money, it didn't matter if she didn't have the transportation. She was going to find a way. Then she confided in me, she had been researching ways to terminate the pregnancy on her own; truly awful, extremely risky ways. It was in this moment, I realized her health was more important than my beliefs and I took her to the clinic. Later that day, I confided in my mom what had happened expecting to be grounded and severely punished. Instead, my Mom shared a similar story. In 1971, her friend in college was pregnant and had a back alley abortion. My mom was the only person she told. We shared our fears on the health of our friends facing an unwanted pregnancy. Although I am strongly pro-choice now that is not what this bill is about for me. Roe v. Wade has not been overturned. This bill is about access and women's health. I am concerned that if this bill passes women all over this state won't have access. I worry about my potential future daughters. I worry about women of low economic means taking severe health risks to exercise their right to choose. I think of my 14 year old friend crumpled in a corner, scared and willing to take matters into her own hands, even if it meant risking her life. Please don't take a step back. Please don't close these doors. Please don't put your personal beliefs before the health of Texas women. Please vote no on HB 60."

This from Ora Houston, Austin, Texas:

"My name is Ora Houston, I am speaking against HB 16 and HB 60 on behalf of myself and my daughter who decided at 30 that she did not want children; her choice, her right. I am against these bills on constitutional and moral grounds. I am an active, faithful Christian in the Episcopal tradition. Let's be clear, the reason we are having this hearing tonight is because elected officials in power, primarily males, are attempting to control the reproductive rights of every female in Texas through legislation, based on their religious dogma and preferences. In my reading of the constitution, the state of Texas is forbidden to legislate based on religious beliefs. In front of us tonight are two such pieces of legislation. I am against these bills on moral grounds. As a child of God, it is my belief that every decision I make about my body, including reproductive choices, is between me and God, not me and politicians, regardless of their faith traditions. Historically, women with limited resources, unlike women of privilege, had one choice; unregulated, unsterile, back room operations. In the years since Roe v. Wade all females have had years of healthy and safe options, including procedures if needed. To seek to limit the rights of females by passing bills which are more limiting, invasive, complicated, complex, and costly is morally reprehensible. What is even more outrageous is that the same legislators who draft and pass these bills, also draft and pass bills which reduce state funding for healthcare, education, mental health services, etc., for the very same babies they were so concerned about in the womb. It appears to me that legislators in power have extreme feelings for the unborn, little if any, for children who are living and breathing outside their mother's womb. The great thing about choice is that females who want to carry their babies to term have that choice and right. And those who don't also have that choice and right. What gives the state of Texas, using thinly veiled language, the right to superimpose their narrow religious beliefs on every female in Texas, entitlement and power."

And this, from Jennifer Jagyellco from Austin, Texas:

"First I would like to thank the chair and the committee for allowing me to testify. My name is Jennifer Jagyellco and I am a constituent of Representative Paul Workman. I'm here today to voice my opposition to the anti-abortion bills HB 16 and HB 60. I realize that you may have already decided how you will vote on these bills. Nevertheless, I respectfully ask that you give me your attention and consider these points. First, if you enact these bills you alienate a growing number of your constituents, including me. I am a registered voter who participates in every election and I will vote against any candidate who is in favor of restricting women's access to abortion. These anti-abortion bills are being presented in the guise of protecting women's health. This is insulting to women's intelligence. Women realize that these bills will not protect their health; they will only reduce their access to abortion providers and limit their ability to make their own medical and family planning decisions. Women and their likeminded partners will continue to be an increasing part of your constituency. Do you really want to alienate them? Second, if you enact these anti-choice bills you risk reducing the talent pool for Texas jobs. Women are a greater portion of professional job candidates than ever before and they now outnumber males in college enrollment. Let me ask you, what young strong-minded independent woman with multiple lucrative job opportunities would want to move to or remain in a state where she has little or no ability to make decisions about her own body and about family planning? How will this effect Texas' ability to create and fulfill jobs? As you know job creation has a point of pride for the governor, his supporters. Third, in order to keep its citizens healthy and productive and to attract more industry Texas needs to have an adequate number of healthcare providers. Increasingly these providers are female. Women now make up nearly half of medical students, up from less than from 25 percent in the 1970's. Females are also the majority of members in The American College of Obstetrics and Gynecology. What female physician with a choice would want to practice in a state where the law severely limits her clinical judgment and her ability to do what she believes is right for her individual patients? How will this effect Texas' ability to attract and maintain an adequate number of medical providers for its population? Before you vote on this anti-abortion bill, I urge you to think carefully about its potential impact on Texas, not just now, but in the future. You have been warned, if you enact these harmful anti-abortion bills be prepared for a mass exodus of talent in Texas. Thank you for your time."

And this, from Jennifer Jaryl McCombs, Austin Texas:

"Dear members of the committee: My name is Jennifer Jaryl McCombs. I'm a fifth generation Austenite and a sixth generation Texan. I'm a mother, a wife, a sister, a daughter, and small business owner. I appreciate the opportunity to be heard by the members of this committee. I am speaking today about the ambulatory surgical centers portion of House Bill 60. It requires all licensed abortion providers' facilities become ambulatory surgical centers. As with most prudent legislation, a problem is identified and a solution is proposed in the form of a bill. The premise of HB 60 assumes that existing abortion facilities are consistently failing or producing poor outcomes to the women who've had an abortion procedure in the state of Texas. The problem: with the acceptance of this premise the argument is to mandate existing abortion clinics to transition their facilities to ambulatory surgical centers. The solution: but this is a solution looking for a problem, the reasoning for the creation of this bill is based on a fallacious foundation, the perceived problem is faulty in that the current regulations, to which existing abortions facilities adhere to are producing exemplary results in the health and safety of their clients. Abortion is one of the safest, surgical procedures for women in the United States. Fewer than .5 percent of women obtaining abortions experience a complication and the risk of death associated with an abortion is about one-tenth of that associated with childbirth. She quotes the Guttmacher institute in saying that. The bottom line is that the current abortion facilities in the state of Texas already operate and perform to high standards. The vast majority of reputable research and patient safety relating to an abortion procedure medical or surgical performed in a licensed facility conclude that favorable outcomes are currently being actualized. Further, HB 60 would create problems for women, financial burdens. This bill would force an existing clinic to either renovate their current facility, purchase an existing ASC if there happens to be one sitting for sale in the clinics area or build a new ASC. Based on the US national average ASC's have an estimated cost of approximately $400 per square foot, including construction costs of $300 a square foot, contractor's fees of about $75 a square foot, and architectural fees of between $32 and $35 a square foot. An ASC can vary in size from 4,000 square feet with one or two operating rooms or to as large as 30,000 to 40,000 square feet, around twelve ORs. Assuming we go with the smallest square footage, 4,000 square feet, we are estimating a total cost to be 1.6 million for that facility. This estimate does not include the purchase of the land, permitting, local, county, or state fees or the cost to provide the additional staff and training required to operate by ASC licensing laws. This is unquestionably a severe and undue financial burden for existing clinics. Access: any of these unreasonable options would be cost prohibitive. It is estimated that of the 42 existing clinics in the state of Texas, only 5 would be able to remain open. That is a greater than 88 percent reduction in access for women in the state of Texas, with the shuttering of these existing proficiently run facilities. Reasonable access is denied to women specifically from the rural areas of Texas. The health and safety of women are not the priority of HB 60. It is with substantial historical context that one could reasonably conclude that women without or with restricted access to abortion providers will still have abortions. Unfortunately they will have to turn back-alley abortions or self-performed abortions. This is a problem. Women in these situations are more likely to have severe complications or die. This problem has already had a solution in the safe and excellent care they receive in the existing abortion facilities as they are currently regulated across Texas. Simply stated, HB 60's origin hinges on the unfounded and unproven proposition that a problem exists for the purposes of maneuvering around a woman's constitutional right for a safe and legal abortion. I respectfully request that the members of this committee take careful consideration to the dramatic consequences that will occur due to the passage of this bill and vote against the passage of HB 60 out of this committee. Please note that the data I referenced in my oral testimony is cited for you in the copies of my written testimony. I mentioned this to contrast the authors of HB 60 and authors of all the abortion restriction bills in the house and the senate who have yet to present a shred of factual data or peer reviewed evidence to support their position on any portion of these bills, despite repeat requests about the regular and special sessions. Thank you."

And she cites the following works for the statistics she gave in her letter: The Guttmacher Institute from 2011, state facts

about abortion, Texas, New York Guttmacher Institute, R.S
Means, 2013, Reed Construction Data, retrieved June 20th,
2013, from its website, Physician's Capitol Investments, 2012,
retrieved June 20th, 2013, from Physician Capitol Investment
website, Planned Parenthood of Greater Texas, 2013, February
25, DSHSAB facilities as of 2-25-2013, 2013 Texas, United
States of America.

And this, from Jane Keytee, who lives in Representative Donna
Duke's district:

"My name is Jane Keytee. I'm here to testify against HB 60
and HB 16. My representative is Donna Dukes. Lieutenant
Governor David Dewhurst bent the rules to add these bills. He
had his chance during the regular session. This should not be
happening, shame on him and shame on you who support these
bills. A woman's body is hers. The state has no right limiting her
healthcare choices including abortion. Abortion is about wom-
en's health, ask any woman whose been diagnosed with cancer at some point in pregnancy, who is given a choice to begin
treatment for cancer and advised to abort her unborn child or
to carry the baby to term with no treatment of the risk she will
die before the baby's due date. Women who have an abortion
do not do so lightly. No woman gets pregnant so she can have
an abortion. Sometimes families end up needing to terminate
a pregnancy, when they thought they never would. These bills
will inordinately affect poor and working poor women. The
clinics that will have to close are not just about abortions. They
provide family counseling, breast exams, pap smears, prenatal
care, and under this bill the abortion pill, which is safe, and
rarely results in complications, will require a before and an after
appointment with a doctor. It also requires a woman to take a
higher dosage than necessary which only indicates the ignorance
of those who wrote these bills. Since it has been shown that
the necessary dosage is much less than the bill would require.
Shame on you who support these bills. Beyond this abortion
bill, it will be challenged in the courts costing an enormous
waste of valuable tax dollars and state resources. We have seen

this in other states, North Dakota and Kansas, where hundreds of thousands to over 1 million dollars and counting of state tax payer money is being spent to defend similar legislations. These anti-women, anti-abortion bills in other states. The bottom line is this, these bills will make abortion harder to obtain and more expensive. As a result, we will see an increase in back alley abortions, self-administered abortions, deaths among women seeking abortions, and unintended pregnancies carried to term. All of which directly create negative public health outcomes and a huge financial drain on the state of Texas. This is not what any of us want for our state, or for our women, children, and families. Shame on you who support these bills. I'm sure your mamas and maybe your grandmamas utter the old adage, 'Be careful what you wish for.' This legislation has raised the ire of thousands upon thousands of women across this state and they vote. Lieutenant Governor Dewhurst and those in the Texas legislature backing these bills need to start planning their retirement. Shame on you, Lieutenant Governor Dewhurst and shame on you who back these bills."

From Lisa LaBlanc in Austin, Texas:

"I stand before you not to protect my reproductive rights. I do not need protection from you any longer. I started menopause at the young age of 27 and at the age of 29 all my reproductive organs were removed. I am a rape survivor. I did not pursue the legal justice I deserve because of fear of the system, and shame and guilt. The shame and guilt I assumed to be mine but we are all well aware it is not. I did everything right. I met this male through a close friend's brother. I spoke with him for a number of hours every other day for 6 weeks before consenting to a date. But when I opened the door to my home, I sensed I was in trouble. I was. I was attacked for over 7 hours in my home. Now they call it date rape. I was paralyzed by fear for 3 years. I was tortured nightly when the phone rang between the hours of 2 and 3 am. The same time the rapist left my house. This occurred nightly for 2 years after the rape. It was just a little daily reminder of what he did and could still do to me. I did turn off the phones closest to my bedroom but I had roommates and they did not know because of shame and I didn't tell anyone for years. They were not aware of why their phones rang nightly; only ringing long enough to remind me who was aware. I stand here before you because you claim to be protecting the safety of women's health issues through passage of these legislative bills. That is a lie. And everyone in this room knows that to be true. The true intention of these bills is to attack a basic human right. The right for any woman in this American society today and I remind you in 2013 and any woman in Texas has the ability to choose her own legal and medically safe choices guaranteed by the Supreme Court of the United States of America. The arguments we hear that support the intention of these bills applies scientific fact and knowledge that these too are lies. There is no factual reason to make these changes. They are introduced and the truth is they will harm access to tens of thousands of women, children, and men to quality healthcare clinics in their rural areas. These bills really are here to target the indigent women of color and their families. And let's be very clear about this fact, you see a room of people with very few faces of color here to represent themselves. They cannot afford to be here. That is why I am here. Do we as a society really understand all the implications of responsibility we assume if we deny a woman's basic human right to choose her own healthcare decisions? If we support HB 60, HB 16, SB 5, then we as a society have to make sure we continue to assume the health and welfare of this woman and the life we expect her to have as these bills become law. Today our society does not impose or focus any reasonable responsibility on these fathers if they are unwed and single mothers. We don't require their involvement or their responsibility to support but the mother's physician or the infant than the child. Our time would be better spent making sure we protect and support mothers and their child's interests and make the father's accountable. And not just financially because we know that raising a child requires so much more than just money. And we all know it is easier with supportive parents. We should be making sure that resources are in place to make this happen not limiting a woman's basic right to choose. If we as a society are going to legislate and take away the basic human right to choose what happens to your own body then we are assuming responsibility that requires those to insure the welfare of both mother and child. We assume responsibility to treat a child's mother with dignity and trust, more trust than what we assumed she did not have in making the right medical decisions for herself, dignity that demonstrates how much we really value a life not causing hardship and harm in the process. Texas actually had legislation this past session concerning childcare for teen parents wanting to complete their high school education and referred to it as rewarding bad behavior. When is deciding to become a parent considered bad behavior? The legislature seem to want it both ways, not allowing the woman's human right to choose what happens to their bodies. Then when they decide to choose what these laws intend. They are not supported but shamed, this not only brings great amounts of shame to the parent but the child as well. It is a stigma that is created for this family by society in general when included in our written laws. Shame damages the soul. It does not create hurt feelings. It causes real damage to who and what that person is and will become. Either we support every aspect of a pregnancy or not. We cannot choose to support after 20 weeks then the first year of life and second and then stop, then we leave it up to the mother to fight for human rights and her child's. We need to provide adequate, affordable, safe healthcare offered within their communities, not like these bills suggest where they must travel hours to find adequate care. You are voting to cause to affect two lives here. This vote requires a lifetime commitment. They imply that more legislation will pass to support and dignify these lives through safe housing, quality healthy food, education in all areas needing attention, affordable daycare, a good efficient transportation system to get to work, stores, daycare, schools, health services and any other services needed. In addition, there will be the emotional costs to keep a child or parent from feeling less than that can lead to addiction, possibly crime, then the cost of treatment. And then there are the possibilities of birth, learning or mental disabilities that continues to add more involvement and support that will be required by us as a society. These are just a few concerns off the top of my head. I'm sure there are many other ramifications from these laws that I've not been able to address. We cannot even provide the education of the children here today that they had in 2010. It is our duty to make sure we are totally responsible for the lives that we impact through our laws. That is the whole reasoning of why we are here, laws are to create justice for all. It is our responsibility to take care of the lives here today. We are failing to accomplish this today. How are we possibly going to be able to include the unseen impact on the lives tomorrow in our failing system? We do not provide what is needed and required as basic human rights for Texas women and children today. They go to bed hungry and wake up hungry. They go to bed sick and wake up sick. They cannot afford shoes, diapers, daycare expenses, and school supplies or a tank of gas. Women and children struggle for daily existence and are not able to come here today and tell what they know to be true. They need support that is not coming. I was taught that a civilization is measured by the way they treat the most vulnerable citizens; the elderly, the sick, the hungry, their children, and their poor. We as a society are failing to provide these measures of basic human needs. Why do you think we're capable of adding more individuals when fiscal responsibilities are not being met today? If these are signed into law where is the money coming from? Where is human decency going to sit? How many basic human rights are going to be left unfulfilled?"

And this from a young woman named April in Austin, Texas:

"Thank you chair and committee members for allowing me to testify. My name is April and I'm a constituent of Representative Don Howard. I'm testifying today to that I am against HB 60. We've heard from senators and representatives here that this bill is to protect patient safety. But we all know after seeing Lieutenant Governor Dewhurst's Twitter account, that isn't the goal at all. The goal of this bill is to limit access to abortion in Texas, which is in blatant opposition to the constitution of these

United States. So let's entertain for a moment, the idea that this bill is actual about patient safety. Humor me, tell me this, if after one year, three years, five years, we find that infection and complication rates fail to improve will the legislature commit to reversing these regulations? Moreover, one of the components of this bill requires that physicians get admitting privileges in local hospitals, never mind that by law hospitals may not refuse treatment of a patient in an emergency condition and never mind that professional organizations like The American College of Obstetricians and Gynecologists and The Texas Hospital Association find this regulation egregious. Bottom line, you are asking these physicians to obtain admitting privileges in facilities where they are unable to practice their specialty. There is no hospital in the state of Texas that will allow an elected pregnancy termination procedure to be performed. I am a lifelong native Texan, as are many generations in my family. I was born here, raised here, committed to obtaining a higher education here, and stayed here to work, even when it might have been easier to move somewhere else where the weather is milder. I am appalled at the sheer audacity of my state government that has chosen to make medical decisions for the physicians and women of Texas, despite most of it senators and representatives not receiving any medical training at all. I am ashamed of my state government who touts low taxes and small government but has chosen to spend more taxpayer money by calling a special session in order to pass laws that have already failed to pass in the regular session. I am disappointed that my state government thinks so poorly of its own citizens that they don't trust them to make their own right decisions for themselves with the advice of their own physicians, their own families, and their own spiritual leaders. Ladies and gentlemen of the House of Representatives, thank you for allowing me to share my testimony today. Please do not pass this harmful, shameful bill."

And this from Jane of Manchaca, Texas:

"My name is Jane. I am here as a mother and grandmother, and a Planned Parenthood volunteer. I grew up in a small Texas town in the 1950's and early '60s. Birth control pills had not been invented and abortion was illegal. There was no sex education in schools, and just as today, girls did get pregnant. If a family had financial means or connections, they might arrange for their daughter to get a safe abortion in a faraway place. Less fortunate girls might find themselves in the hands of a shady, illegal abortionist and suffer the consequences of injury or death. Many found themselves in sudden marriages at an early age. They found themselves trapped in unhappy marriages or living a hard life as a single mother, shamed in a community, without education, with hard, low paying jobs. I was right here in this capitol, in March 1972, when women filled the halls to lobby for the equal rights amendment. Even though the federal legislation failed to gain national ratification, I was proud that Texas was among the states that stood up for the rights of women. We have come a long way since then. Birth control and access to safe legal abortion have changed the lives of women, men, and families. I have a friend who faced a very difficult choice a few years ago. She and her husband were expecting a baby that they very much wanted. They were so excited. Then genetic tests revealed that the child was carrying a specific gene that is common to serial killers, not all persons with this gene become serial killers, but many serial killers share the gene. What a terrible choice to make. Do you bring into the world a person who might someday kill the loved ones of others? Do you trust God to take care of everything? I won't tell you what choice they made. It's no one's business and that is the point. How can the state of Texas assert itself into such a difficult private dilemma? There has been a lot of dissembling about the purposes of this legislation being to make the healthcare safer for women. I salute our Lieutenant Governor for his honesty yesterday in Tweeting the truth; that the purpose of this legislation is to end abortion in Texas. It makes me very sad as a sixth generation Texan to see my home state moving back to the 1950's. I've seen the 1950's and I don't want to go back there. I ask that you oppose HB 60. Thank you for your time."

And this from Carol in Austin, Texas:

"No one ever thinks they're going to be faced with a decision of terminating a much wanted pregnancy or deciding when to shut off the life support of their beloved child. My spouse and I were faced with exactly that decision. On December 1st, 2008, I was thrilled to discover that I was pregnant with my first child. My husband and I had recently married and decided to start having kids right away. Four months later we went in for a regularly scheduled ultrasound at 20 weeks where we were going to find out if we were having a boy or a girl. Finding out your baby's sex is easily the most exciting time of any pregnancy. And we were ecstatic to discover that we were having a girl. Unfortunately, that moment was cut short when the OB/GYN also told us that our baby was sick and referred us to the maternal fetal specialist. Two days later we were given the heartbreaking news that our daughter was not only sick, but had a terminal condition, hydrops fatalis, in which an abnormal amount of fluid build-up in the body. Given the early onset of my daughter's illness, her condition was very grave and we left the specialist's office with our choices. We could wait until she passed, induce my labor, or have a dilation and extraction. Knowing that your daughter is dying is heartbreaking. When you are given the news that there is nothing that can be done to save your baby's life it feels like your soul has been ripped apart, but we had a decision to make. Even if we decided not to do anything, we were still making a decision and we had a limited amount of time to decide. There were so many things to consider. Did I want to hold my baby? Did I want to name her? Did I want to have her baptized? Where would she be buried? Would I be able to hold her while she died? If she somehow did survive until term. In the meantime, I couldn't eat, I couldn't sleep, and I couldn't leave the house. Every time that I left the house someone would comment on my pregnancy. They asked perfectly normal questions about my due date, the gender, the name. I answered their questions as nicely as I could and then I would turn around and burst into tears. So eventually I stopped leaving my house. I couldn't eat because my stomach was in knots from the anxiety. I didn't know exactly what was going to happen and I didn't know when it would happen and I definitely couldn't sleep. I was petrified that my baby was going to die while I was asleep. I just knew that I was going to wake up one day, and discover that she had died at some point during the night. The idea that I couldn't be with her and know when she had passed was more than I could bear. We decided to have my labor induced. It felt like the best path for our family. I started making burial arrangements. We didn't have a grave plot for her because we never anticipated needing one. Instead of planning a nursery, I was picking out a headstone for my baby. Instead of choosing outfits for her to wear home, I was picking out her burial gown. It was devastating but there was some comfort in the fact that we were moving forward. Except we weren't really moving forward, shortly after making our decision, to have my labor induced, we were informed that it wasn't really possible. My husband worked for Seaton at the time, so we had Seaton insurance. As a faith based organization, Seaton would not allow us to have our labor induced while our daughter still had a heartbeat. That meant that we were either forced to wait until she passed or agree to have her heart stopped. After weeks of being crippled by grief and anxiety, I couldn't imagine waiting any longer. Our obstetrician appealed to the ethics board at Seaton, on our behalf but our appeal was denied. So we made the decision to have our daughter's heart stopped. In the meantime, I prayed and begged for a miracle. A miracle that I knew wasn't coming. Every night I would talk to my baby, who we named Amber Grace and I would tell her that I loved her. I would tell her that I loved her and that I was sorry that she was sick and then I would tell her that it was okay to leave me. At this point my daughter was going to die. It was only a matter of time. When and where it happened, and if we could avoid having her heart stopped, then that is what we prayed for. But she didn't die on her own. On April 8th, 2009, we went to the specialist's office, 5 pm, we took a final look at our baby on the screen, said our goodbyes, and her heart was stopped less than an hour later. My labor was induced that night, and she was delivered four years ago, on April 9th. I held her, kissed her, watched her get baptized, told her that I loved her and I said goodbye. None of our daughter's life and death went as planned or expected. I expected to have her for the rest of my life and when that wasn't possible, I expected to be able to say goodbye to her in the way that I had chosen but that wasn't possible either. It is very frustrating to feel like the choices you have made for your baby's life and death are not being respected. Hearing that your baby is going to die, makes everything in your life feel like it's out of your control. Being told that you don't really have any control over how your baby is going to die is devastating and self defeating. I chose to have a baby and bring her into this world. I should be allowed to make the very personal, very private, and very painful decision as to how she leaves it, guided by the best interest of my child and my family. If a 20 week ban had been in place four years ago, then I wouldn't have been able to make this choice. Waiting for your child to pass is certainly a viable option for many who have been in my position, but so is the path that I chose and would choose again. Physically, I faced a small chance of developing complications from continuing to carry her while she was sick. Mentally and emotionally, however, I would have deteriorated and mental illness can be just as debilitating as physical illness. I would hate to see other families not have the right to choose what is best for them. These decisions are hard enough without placing extra limits on them."

From Geraldine in Austin, Texas:

"I am representing myself and faith action for women in need and I am against HB 60. Mr. Chairman, you tell me that you have treated me and the others here with respect. Sir, I know exactly what respect looks like. Respect is not calling a special session in order to ram anti-choice legislation through the legislature. Respect is not closing most of the abortion clinics in the state and calling it an improvement in women's health. Respect is not trying to create a de facto ban on abortion, when safe and legal abortion is supported by the clear majority of Texans. Respect is not burning up the three minutes people are allowed to speak with your own reiteration of the procedures, or grandstanding, or cutting them off before their time is up. Respect is not wandering in and out of the chamber when men and women tell the most intimate stories of their lives. Respect is not shoving an ultrasound wand inside a woman's vagina for a painful medical unnecessary state-mandated rape because she should have the bad fortune to need an abortion, or even because she is miscarrying her wanted child. I grew up in a Texas that had scientifically accurate sex education. I grew up in a Texas where a well-equipped and fully-funded Planned Parenthood was around the corner to provide the high-quality healthcare and family planning that an uninsured teenager needed to ensure she could manage her fertility and make her own choices in life. I used to be so proud of being a Texan, but now I am ashamed. When friends tell me 'If you've got a uterus, you've got to leave that state,' I have to agree that they speak the truth. I fear for my daughter's future in a state that values the right to carry a gun on the college campus she attends over her right, not just to bodily integrity and choice, but her right to life itself. Because HB 60, if enacted, will cause even more deaths of Texas women already suffering from cuts to women's health programs and the failure of this state to expand Medicaid coverage. This bill is a hateful attack on Texas women and their families and must not be enacted."

From Peggy, in Austin, Texas:

"Dear Texas House Affairs Chair and Committee, I signed up to speak Thursday at the committee hearing about 1 P.M. and was never allowed to speak even though I waited ten and a half hours and listened to many a male speaker who'd signed up after I did. Please accept this copy of my testimony. I appreciate your service and open ear to my story about why I'm testifying against both HB 16 and 60. I'm Peggy from District 48, represented by the honorable and wise Representative Donna Howard. If y'all would listen to her intelligent input, I wouldn't need to be here speaking to you today, and I could be out volunteering as usual to help immigrants learn English, the homeless get fed, and poor kids find affordable tutoring during the summer. I'm a retired public school teacher currently volunteering as chair of the Social Action Committee of First Unitarian Universalist Church of Austin, which means I represent about 200 voting adults from the Austin area. When I talk about how backwards you're leaning by proposing House Bills 16 and 60, I'm opposed to these bills and I'm perplexed about why you're wasting time on these bills that are not pro-life at all but only designed to prevent women from getting needed healthcare. You could better spend your time by looking at ways to help our many unwanted children in Texas, not to mention helping the many women in this state who live in poverty because your laws have not fully funded education, women's healthcare, or family planning. Sure, you made up for some of the funding that was cut two years ago, but you know you have more work to do. Instead, you're coming up with more ways to cost taxpayer money and limit women's healthcare. Every human, no matter what age, should be wanted. Yet, I'm watching Texas politicians interfere with the healthcare decisions that should be between a woman, her family and her doctor. Lawmakers, either get out of the vagina business or go to medical school. Regarding HB 16, why did you come up with a generic ban on an abortion after 20 weeks when doctors sometimes learn new information later than that and abortions are legal for up to 24 to 28 week? I'd say that if you vote for this bill, you're simply happy to ignore medical science and watch women and children die for no reason. I know it shouldn't surprise me, since you sit back regularly and watch people killed via capital punishment. Many of our inmates sitting on death row were once unwanted babies, and what have you done for them? Anyone who calls this a 'fetal pain' bill is forgetting the pain of life. Granted, this fetus will miss the good life, which could be if the fetus were fortunate enough to be born into a family with money. What about being forced into the pain of poverty and sexual discrimination? Think of the pain many women and children live with today which you could eradicate with an open mind and heart. Why aren't you working to pass laws to educate our teens about human sexuality? Only four percent of Texas school districts teach our teens about responsible pregnancy, contraception, and disease prevention, according to the *Dallas Morning News*. That's outrageous. And you know it if you've been paying attention because Texas has one of our nation's highest teen pregnancy rates and second-highest teen birth rates. What are you doing for these moms, families and children? Why aren't you working more for our children to have health insurance and care? Additionally, HB 60 is absurd because it places unnecessary requirements on health centers, which will reduce abortion facilities from 42 to 5. While women with money will still be able to get abortions, you will assure more poor women of either bringing their unwanted babies in the world to be malnourished, unsupported and uneducated, or it'll send them to the fatal abortionist who existed when I first went to college in 1972. Are you really okay with more coat hangers? A vote for this bill says you are. If I saw y'all working to truly support our many children living in poverty or in the broken foster care system, I wouldn't consider you pro-death, but that is exactly how I will see any of you who vote for this horrific legislation. Please, in the name of humanity, vote no on HB 16 and 60."

And this from Amy from Austin, Texas:

"Thank you to the Chair and the Committee for allowing me to testify. My name is Amy and I am a constituent of Representative Elliot Naishtat from Austin. I am here representing myself. I am also a volunteer with the Lilith Fund, an abortion assistance fund which speaks directly to low-income women needing abortion care but unable to access it because of cost, distance, and many other reasons. I am here to testify against HB 16 and HB 60 because it is important that abortion remain legal, safe, and accessible for all Texas women. I had an abortion when I was 23. I was unemployed and suffering from health problems. My life wasn't stable enough to provide a home for a child and my health wasn't sturdy enough to continue a pregnancy. I had to borrow money for the abortion but I was fortunate enough to live close to a clinic. My abortion was safe and professional and I recovered from it quickly. However, my abortion was a wake-up call. I decided that if I were to get pregnant again, I wanted to be in a better position to have a healthy pregnancy and provide a stable home for a child. I got a job that led to a career. I went to grad school and I worked on improving my health. As it turns out, I've never gotten pregnant again, but in the course of dealing with my health issues, I discovered that I have a genetic condition. It isn't fatal, but it does lead to a decreased life expectancy, a decreased quality of life, and a far greater chance of developing major, fatal diseases. The worst part of it is the constant, chronic pain that this condition causes. No matter the treatment or how well I take care of myself, I have to live with constant, chronic pain, which gets worse every year. If I were to get pregnant again, I could not imagine sentencing a child to a life of constant, chronic pain due to some bad genes—my bad genes. While I take every precaution to make sure that I don't get pregnant, birth control sometimes fails and rapes sometimes happen. If I were to get pregnant again, I would have an abortion. Despite having a master's degree, despite having a good job and health insurance, despite being able to provide a stable and loving home for a child. It is my hope for every woman who is not able or willing to continue a pregnancy for whatever reason that she can have access to a safe, professional and legal abortion, but if these bills pass, it will guarantee the end of safe, professional, accessible and legal abortion for a large number of Texas women. These bills put undue burdens on women and these bills will prevent women from being able to choose what is best for them, their health, their families and their futures. Please do not vote for HB 16 and HB 60. Thank you."

This from Alyssa who lives in District 45, Representative Jason Isaac, District 25, Senator Donna Campbell:

"My name is Alyssa and I would like to testify against House Bill 60 because it will restrict abortion in arbitrary and unnecessary ways, ways that I fear are motivated to keep women from pursuing challenging, competitive careers. Now would quite possibly be the worst time for me to become a mother, the worst time for me as well as my possible child. I have worked to get my first degree and to build the beginning of a career as a professor, however, this career will take a lot more time and effort to get it off the ground. I am about to get my M.A. and hopefully PhD., which will take from six to eight years to complete. During these years, I will have to work tirelessly and for very little money. It will take all of the energy and time I have to make it through this period. If I do make it through this, and successfully get onto the tenure track job market, my success will be far from guaranteed. I will still have to campaign tirelessly to get hired, probably for several years, and possibly work several jobs as an adjunct, positions that often pay significantly less than the salaries of high school teachers in the state of Texas and allow faculty little time to do the research they really care about. But if I do eventually get the job I want, the job I know I'm more than qualified to get, I will be able to do what I love for the rest of my life: to do research that is important, that will inspire students the way I have been inspired by my own professors. Getting pregnant could very well ruin this dream, especially if I do not have the choice to end the pregnancy. If I had to drive far away because all of the clinics near my university have been closed, adding the expense of gas to the expense of the procedure itself, abortion could rendered prohibitively expensive for me. If I had a child, I would likely be changing diapers instead of writing my dissertation and devoting all of my money to paying babysitters rather than traveling to deliver papers at a conference. If I do not make it through, I will have to take whatever probably low-paying job my bachelor's degree in English can get me, a job that would not likely ever be able to provide adequately for myself, much less a child, even when combined with my partner's salary. Though I am certainly taking precautions against getting pregnant, if I did happen to get pregnant, I would want to know that I had the option of choosing to end that pregnancy. Choosing abortion would be difficult for me. I am not pro-abortion; I am pro-choice. However, knowing that I had a choice would make it possible for me to come to a decision that I felt at peace with, a decision that I could at least say was my own. Every woman deserves this choice. The Texas legislature is attempting to claim that this choice is really their own, bullying women not located near urban areas into becoming mothers. This will likely result in many individual women losing the kind of economic and social power that full control over their reproductive lives makes possible for them now. It will keep them from being extraordinary. This is not even to mention the fact that many will likely be prevented from excelling because they will be dead from the many—from the badly-done illegal abortions they will begin to seek when their access to legal abortion is restricted. The Texas Legislature is proving that it has the power to push women into subordinate positions and even to kill them. During this special session, the Texas Legislature had proved that it can do whatever it chooses, up to and including silencing the peoples' testimonies on this issue as they did in the State Affairs Committee on June 20th. Unfortunately for the Texas Legislature, their power comes from the people's votes, which cannot be silenced. Half of these votes will come from women who will make sure that the next time a special session like this is called, it is filled with representatives who will value and attempt to protect their reproductive rights."

And this from Melissa in Austin, Texas:

"Thank you chair and committee for allowing me to testify. I am Melissa, a constituent of Representative Dukes and mommy to Iris, who is six, and Sam, who is four. I am here to testify against HB 16 and the anti-abortion bills because there are thousands of reasons women make the choice to have an abortion procedure, so many more than rape, incest, and the life of the mother. What happens to a woman's body should not be legislated. HB 16 only makes an exception for the life of the mother and does not make an exception for fetal abnormalities. 0.57 percent of the abortions in Texas are after 20 weeks, almost half of one percent. The women who receive abortions after 20 weeks make this painful decision with their families, usually after receiving news that their child has such severe abnormalities and would only be able to live outside of the womb for minutes, hours, or days, and that their child would die, possibly in extreme pain.

These pregnancies are wanted, planned and loved. The idea of fetal pain is being used as the excuse to outlaw abortion after 20 weeks. The *Journal of the American Medical Association* found evidence that the brain connectors to feel pain are not formed until at least 24 weeks. I think we should use evidence found by the American Medical Association rather than an article in *USA Today* that Representative Laubenberg read on a plane. What about the mental and emotional pain of these parents and the physical pain their child may be in from being born before their pending death? Do you think that you, the lawmakers, have the right to make these women carry and then watch their babies suffer and die? How long is too long to watch your baby suffer before it dies? One minute? One hour? One day? Taking this choice away from these women is gut-wrenching and wrong. We are women, we are mothers, daughters, and most importantly, we are human beings. Trust us to make decisions about our bodies and our health decisions with our doctors. Thank you."

This from Pamela in Round Rock, Texas, District 52, Representative Larry Gonzales. This was her planned testimony on HB 16:

"I registered to testify on HB 60 and HB 16 and waited for more than ten hours to be called to testify on HB 60. I was denied the right to do so. After shutting down testimony on HB 60, Chairman Cook then decided to arbitrarily and severely restrict the number of witnesses allowed to testify on HB 16, thus preventing Representatives from hearing from me and hundreds of other Texans. My prepared testimony against HB 16 follows: Thank you chair and committee for allowing me to testify. My name is Pamela. I live and vote in Round Rock. I am a constituent of Representative Larry Gonzales in District 52. I am here today to testify against House Bill 16, the proposed measure that would ban abortions after 20 weeks. Since the legalization of abortion in 1973, abortion services have become more widely accessible. As a result, the overwhelming majority of abortions are performed in the first trimester of pregnancy. For a number of reasons, however, abortion after the first trimester remains a necessary option for women. Although the proponents of HB 16 might say otherwise, their goal is to ban all abortions and severely restrict the right of women to control their own bodies. They call themselves 'pro-life,' but in fact they threaten violence against doctors and endanger the health of women and the right of physicians to determine the most appropriate treatment for their patients. Their arguments about so-called fetal pain and similar unfounded and fear-based claims are rehashes of decades of old rhetoric. Combined with HB 60 and provisions in SB 5, HB 16 concocts a perfect storm that endangers the women of Texas and bars their access to abortion. Factors that force women to have abortions after the first trimester include barriers to service, provider shortages, cost, and legal restrictions. Other reasons include psychological denial of pregnancy as occurs in cases of rape or incest, lack of financial support, lack of pregnancy symptoms, and the seeming continuation of monthly menstrual periods or irregular periods. Medical indications affecting pregnancy may also lead to abortion after the first trimester. Some of these include fetal health concerns from a lack of prenatal care, fetal exposure to prescription medications and fetal anomaly due to advanced maternal age. Existing conditions in which a woman's health is threatened or aggravated by continuing her pregnancy include certain types of infections, health failure, malignant hypertension including pre-eclampsia, out of control diabetes, serious renal disease, severe depression, and suicidal ideation. These and other symptoms may not occur until the second trimester or they may become worse as the pregnancy progresses. In Roe v. Wade, the U.S. Supreme Court held that the U.S. Constitution protects a woman's personal decision to end a pregnancy. Only after viability, being capable of sustained survival outside a woman's body, with or without artificial aid, may states ban abortion altogether. Abortions necessary to preserve a woman's life or health must still be allowed, however, even after viability. HB 16, like its companion bill HB 60, is not pro-life. It is an anti-woman's health measure that endangers the women of Texas and interferes with personal decisions between women and their doctors. I urge you to reject HB 16."

And this from Melissa in Austin:

"Thank you chair and committee for allowing me to testify. My name is Melissa and I am a constituent of Representative Mark Strama of District 50. I am here to testify against HB 60 because I believe in the equality of women and reproductive justice. In 1978 I had an abortion. I had that surgical abortion in a doctor's office and felt completely cared-for and safe. It was a very difficult decision for me, and the right decision. I am grateful I lived in a state where my rights as a woman and a citizen of the United States of America were respected. I was allowed to make the best choice for me and my family. I could give you a list of reasons why I did what I did but the truth is that those reasons are private and none of your, or anyone else's, business. I don't have to defend my decision. It was my right to make it and should always be the right of every individual woman. No one else could possibly know my mind, my heart, or understand why I made the choice I did. And they don't have to. My rights to make decisions about my own body are mine to make, just as you have the right to make your own decisions about your health, your body, your well-being. Why do you deny my freedom of choice? The idea that doctors would need admitting privileges at a hospital within 30 miles is ridiculous. There are many places in this state where there is not a hospital within 30 miles of the community. Why are you not concerned with the health of those Texans? And what about women giving birth? More women have complications and die in childbirth than from abortion, shouldn't supporting small community hospitals be a priority? If you really cared about life, and reducing the number of abortions, wouldn't expanding Medicaid, providing science-based sex education, easy access to birth control, funding Planned Parenthood, and doing all you could—all you could to make healthcare available to each child, woman and man in Texas be your focus? If all you want to do is be pro-birth, then claim that. I hear that you claim a religious basis for you actions, yet I see no legislation reflecting compassion for the children in Texas that go to bed hungry each night, or the children that are abused, abandoned and neglected. I see no legislation providing easy access to birth control to reduce the need for abortion. I see no legislation to provide for childcare, a living minimum wage, or family leave so more women would feel that they could care for a child. I am against this assault on my rights and the basic equality of women. Reproductive rights are central to women's equal rights and autonomy in society. Men are free to use and buy birth control at any age. Men are free to have vasectomies, or not. And if they impregnate someone, they are not required to subsume their rights and the sovereignty over their own bodies at the directive of another person's religious beliefs. Freedom of choice means that every woman and man is free to make personal decisions about their reproductive lives based on their own religious beliefs and consciences."

And this from Ellen in Austin, Texas:

"Hello, thank you for allowing me to testify. My name is Ellen and I reside in Rollingwood, Texas, House District 48, Representative Donna Howard's district. I am testifying against HB 60. As a person of faith, as a Jew, I am dismayed that some religious views are not being taken into account and respected, as this bill aims to make it more and more difficult for a woman to have access to abortion care. My faith is clear on this issue. My Jewish values state that every woman has a right to self-determination, and Judaism views the well-being of the mother as paramount, placing the highest value on existing life. My faith-based perspective informs me whether to terminate a pregnancy as a deeply personal and immensely complex decision, one that should be left to the woman in consultation with her doctor, her partner, her religious values, and her conscience. The bill being heard today represents an intrusion on these values. It seems more aimed to shame a woman than to support her, to treat an individual as if she cannot make and carry out this most important personal decision as her own moral guide. Too often we suppose to know what is in the heart of another person, but of course we all know that that is not possible, so I ask the members of this committee not to dictate a decisions such as this for another person. Do not suppose to know what is truly in the heart of a woman who is seeking an abortion, particularly one who is perhaps a victim of rape or incest. I urge the members of this committee to vote against these bills and keep abortion care safe, legal, and accessible for the women of Texas. Thank you for the opportunity."

And this from Julie in Pflugerville, Texas:

"Good afternoon. Thank you, chair and committee for allowing me to testify, my name is Julie, and I am a constituent of Representative Mark Strama. I am here to testify against these bills because I believe that the intent of these bills is to try to further restrict access to safe abortion care. I believe that our ability as women to make personal reproductive choices in the future will be in jeopardy if these bills are passed. I am currently employed at Austin Women's Health Center, and I have worked there for more than eight years. We pride ourselves on providing high-quality reproductive care to the women of central Texas. From my experience working in an abortion clinic, I know firsthand that abortion is an incredibly safe procedure. I have yet to hear or read about any data or studies that report to the contrary, and my own personal experience working in a clinic has been that the complication rate is incredibly low. Excessive regulations of abortion care are already in place in this state. We are regulated, and subject to inspections by the Department of State Health Services, the Texas Medical Board, the Clinical Laboratory Improvement Amendments, the National Abortion Federation, and various insurance companies. I am concerned that requiring all abortions be performed in ambulatory surgical center is extreme and unnecessary, and will in effect result in abortion being less safe by causing women to resort to illegal and unsafe methods to protect—or to end their pregnancies. It is incredibly worrisome to me to think that any women . . . any woman . . . in need of an abortion service, whether it is elective or therapeutic, may only have five clinics in the entire state to choose from if these laws are passed. We encounter women at our clinic on a daily basis that already face difficulty arranging transportation to our office, even when they live in the area. Many women will not be able to afford the financial burden associated with increased transportation costs. Delays in receiving treatment due to patient overload of the few remaining clinics may result in women having to wait until the second trimester to be seen. At that point the financial cost and medical risk begin to increase exponentially. If you really care about women's safety, you will vote no to this bill. The need for safe abortion care in our community will not go away if this bill is passed. Women will not stop seeking abortion services. What will be different, though, is we will lack legitimate, regulated health centers that provide high-quality medical care to women, because this bill will drive legitimate providers, such as the one that I work for, out of the practice. I have witnessed thousands of women walk through our doors seeking abortion services, each with their own unique story to tell. These women are from every walk of life, every age bracket, every race, ethnicity, every income level, every education level, and every religion. They all choose abortion because they believe in their hearts that it is the best decision for them in their situation, and we trust them. I encourage you all to also trust them to make these medical decisions with the least amount of government interference. Thank you."

From Martha, in Luling, Texas:

"I am Martha, I live in Tim Kleinschmidt's District 17, I represent myself in absolute opposition to HB 60. Today I am here to speak out for Texas women, for the least of those among us. I want my voice to count for something tonight, because for two years I have watched as my state leaders have leveled attack after attack on women's healthcare, from slashing funds for family planning services and wellness exams to de-funding Planned Parenthood. I have seen with my own eyes what these cuts have done to women in my own community. My heart is breaking. As a concerned citizen, I have done what I am supposed to do when I disagree with my state government. I've made phone calls to Mr. Kleinschmidt, to my state senator, Judith Zaffirini, and to the governor's office. I have written letters to them, letters to the editors of many newspapers, and even protested on many occasions at the capital. Yet, nothing has changed. I want my voice to count. On Tuesday night, during the Senate hearing on SB 5, I listened as Senators Patrick, Deuell, Nelson, and the bill's author, Glenn Hagar, claimed that this action is pro-women's health. In my estimation, nothing could be further from the truth. If Texas is truly about the business of being pro-women's health, then shouldn't we start by fully restoring funds to the women's health program and the forfeited Title 10 funds? Shouldn't we see to it that there's a Planned Parenthood in every community in this state? Shouldn't we expand Medicaid so that more women can enjoy access to healthcare? If we are really pro-women's health, then we must ensure that all Texas women have access to education, to birth control, to options. This bill and HB 16 take away my options. These bills were dead at the close of regular session. I believe our Lieutenant Governor bent the rules to get them on the fast track of this special session. That we are even here today fighting the passage of the bills is an outrage. We now know, because of his irresponsible Tweet on Wednesday morning, that Dewhurst's goal is to close all clinics in Texas that provide abortion services, and we are not amused. In 2011 our legislature passed the sonogram law, with nary an outcry from the public. Not this time. There are thousands of other citizens of this state who are unable to be here in person tonight, who will fight every affront to Texas women's reproductive freedom. I want you to know that if this state's elected officials continue to wage war on women in my state, I will do everything in my power to work toward their defeat. I am Martha. Let the record show that I vehemently oppose HB 60. Thank you."

From Kayleigh, in Austin, Texas:

"I am here today to speak for myself and to voice my opposition to this legislation. I am opposed, as a social worker, a healthcare professional, an abortion provider, and as a woman. I will not abide when others try to legislate away my rights by creating undue and unnecessary restrictions on a legal, medical procedure. I do not want to live in a place where women are not trusted to make private decisions for themselves without legislative interference. I believe that decreasing access to abortion for political and religious reasons is bad—an unconstitutional health policy. It does not serve to protect the health and safety of women. Limiting access to an already safe medical procedure, indeed, safer than carrying a pregnancy to term, will force women into unsafe, at-home abortions, or into the arms of unscrupulous people who take advantage of desperate women. Lastly and most importantly, I trust women to decide what is best for them, and that includes access to abortion on demand, and without apology. Thank you."

And this from Victoria, in Buda Texas:

"Hello, my name is Victoria, and I'm here today as a concerned Texas resident opposing HB 16 and HB 60, and as a constituent of Representative Jason Isaac. My story is one of traditional success. Teenage girl makes it all the way through high school with great grades, gets into an elite college, works at a job she loves, and regularly educates herself on the politics of her state and nation. But I am lucky. I am not special; I have not lived my life any differently than many of the women who have sought abortions in this state. The decision to terminate one's own pregnancy is an incredibly personal, medical decision, and it is one that we have a constitutional right to, as Americans. The bills on the floor tonight represent a belief in this country that the women who seek abortions are shameful, careless, liars, who do not have the mental capacity to make these decisions for themselves. As a young woman, I find that belief to be abhorrent, not to mention insulting, and dead wrong. The women who have sought and continue to seek abortions are just like me: women who are successful, compassionate, smart, and capable human beings. I am fortunate that I have not had to make the heart-wrenching decision to end a pregnancy, but that is not because I am somehow better than the women who have had to face that decision. The rhetoric used to shame women who seek these services is intentionally designed to scapegoat them so that they become dehumanized in the eyes of the media and its consumers. If women who seek abortions are characterized as reckless and immoral, it is easy to strip them of their rights, dignity, and humanity. It seems ironic, then, that in order to save the humanity of a fetus, grown adults must dehumanize and restrict the rights of women. If we assume that this rhetoric is not just rhetoric, and a true belief held by those who are anti-choice, how can they justifiably argue that the women who are seeking abortions, and whom they believe to be incompetent, should carry to term, give birth to, and raise a human being? We must begin to speak honestly and compassionately about and for women and our experiences. Because the choices that we make, the lives we live, and the children we do or do not bring into the world deserve more respect than the current rhetoric surrounding women's health. In conclusion, HB 16 and HB 60 are not just a danger to women's physical health, but to their mental health, to their self-image, to their public image, and to their general dignity. I am speaking against them as a young woman, a young woman who reserves the right to make decisions about my body, my mental health, and my capabilities. I do not believe that the Texas legislature has the right to make decisions about what healthcare I have access to, or the personal decisions that I am or am not allowed to make. As a woman, as a human being, and as a constituent of the state of Texas, I oppose these bills. Thank you for your time."

And this from Danielle, from Austin, Texas:

"Many disagree about politics. But so many that I run into will agree, regardless of political affiliation, that it's difficult to fully love others if a person doesn't love herself. Similarly, it's hard to help or care for others without being able to do it for oneself first. That's why on airplanes they always tell the adults to put on an oxygen mask before the child's. What good is the adult to the child if the adult is suffocating? In December of 1973, my mother was 18 and living in Amarillo, Texas. She conceived my half-sister, Abby, with a man she did not know well, who she felt affection for but did not love. She knew she was not ready for a baby; she made almost no money and had unresolved PTSD from sexual and emotional abuse. But her family was going to disown her if she put the child up for adoption. I can only imagine . . . Texas was similar to what it might be like if this bill passed. Abortion was technically legal, but not very accessible. She had the option to be further shunned by her family, or to have the baby. When Abby was four years old, she was diagnosed with leukemia, which she lived with until she was twelve years old. She passed away in my mother's arms while she was giving her a sponge bath. Abby's leukemia was the result of growing up next to a nuclear power plant, and jet fuel line from an Air Force base. So how are we to expect mothers to not seek out abortions when our government shows no interest in stopping the contributions to toxicity in our environment, while simultaneously encouraging families to control their daughters' bodies, while simultaneously doing so little to help those who are victims of sexual violence, and domestic abuse? My mother does not regret raising Abby, despite the trauma of eventually losing her. But she regrets that she grew up in a time where she had so little agency about a choice she needed to make herself—not her family, not her government. She believes as a result of her struggle, and so taught me, that all women need options. I ask the government and people in favor of this bill why they are so concerned with the fetus, but not the four-year-olds who are in toxic environments, who may not have access to healthy food, or any food at all? Why are they so convinced that a mother can properly care for another human being when the world puts up so many barriers for her to even take care of herself? If you value the life of a child, you must value the life of the woman who carries it. If you value the life of a child, then you need to value their entire life, not just when they are a collection of cells in a uterus. If you want to blame a woman for not wanting to bring a child in the world, I suggest making it better . . . a better, an easier world to raise the children we already have, who are struggling to thrive because of environmental decay and economic disparity. However, I suggest not blaming the woman at all, for you are likely to never be in her shoes."

From Jane in Austin:

"To the chair and committee members: my name is Jane, I am here to testify against HB 60 and HB 16, my representative is Donna Dukes. Lieutenant Governor David Dewhurst bent the rules to add these bills. He had his chance during the regular session; this should not be happening. Shame on him and shame on you who support these bills. A woman's body is hers. The state has no right limiting her healthcare choices, including abortion. Abortion is about women's health, ask any woman who has been diagnosed with cancer at some point in a pregnancy, who is given a choice to begin treatment for cancer and advised to abort her unborn child, or to carry the baby to term with no treatment, at the risk she will die before the baby's due date. Women who have an abortion do not do so lightly. No woman gets pregnant so she can have an abortion. Sometimes families end up needing to terminate a pregnancy when they never thought they would. These bills will inordinately affect poor and poor working women. The clinics that will have to close are not just about abortion; they provide family counseling, breast exams, pap smears, prenatal care. And under this bill, the abortion pill, which is safe, and rarely results in complications, will require a before and an after appointment with a doctor. It also requires a woman to take a higher dosage than necessary, which only indicates the ignorance of those who wrote these bills, since it's been shown that the necessary dosage is much less than the bill would require. Shame on you who support these bills. The omnibus abortion bill will be challenged in the courts, causing an enormous waste of valuable tax dollars and state resources. We've seen this in other states. The bottom line is this: these bills will make abortion harder to obtain, and more expensive. And as a result, we will see an increase in back alley abortions, self-administered abortions, deaths among women seeking abortions, and unintended pregnancies carried to term, all of which directly create negative public health outcomes and a huge financial drain on the state of Texas. This is not what any of us want for our state, or for our women, children, and families. Shame on you who support these bills."

This is from Linea in Austin.

"Thank you, chair and committee, for allowing me to testify. My name is Linea, and I am a constituent of Representative Donna Dukes, and I'm here to testify against bills SB 5, HB 60, and HB 16. Mr. Chairman, I will gladly share my personal story with you if you feel that it will contribute to this hearing, and that you have the time and patience to listen to it through to the end. It is not very long, but it is longer than three minutes. Not too long ago, I became unexpectedly pregnant. Now, I've lived a fairly easy life. When I became pregnant, at the time I lived in a house owned by my family, I was 30 years old, married to the man I've been with for over a decade, relatively stable income; all the factors that one thinks one needs in order to raise a family. And yes, at first we decided to sustain the pregnancy. We even told our parents and some friends. And then, the panic set in for me. I became overwhelmed with emotions. I tried to keep them at bay, but when I found myself resisting the urge to wish for a miscarriage, I knew I had made . . . I knew I had to make a different choice. I could not find the strength within me, but when I went to my husband, and that wonderful man took my hand and said, 'You don't need to make this alone, I will make it with you. We will make this choice together.' What changed? I'm a person that loves life, honors life so much that I don't even eat animals. I wish for there to be as little suffering as possible in this world. But in those days of moving toward a choice of abortion, the reality of my situation became crystal clear, as if I were going through a near-death experience. You see, my family discovered when I was very . . . my family divorced when I was very young. My parents, the two people who brought me into this world, hated each other. I do not remember a time seeing them show love for each other. My concept of love had been, for so long, related to abandonment, to loss, to hate. How could I expect my child to love in a healthy way if I did not myself know how to love? Three other factors were the same as this: How could I expect my child to deal with anger and negativity if I did not know how? How could I expect my child to embrace its creative expression and follow its heart if I did not know how? How could I expect my child to be physically healthy and respect their body if I did not know how? These four things were irrefutable to me; I could not be the parent that I feel every child deserves without these factors in place. Even though the idea of abortion was, and still is, heartbreaking to me, bringing up a child with these disadvantages was even more painful. Throughout my pregnancy, all the way through my abortion, I did not drink or take my migraine medication—my little way of showing that I value life, even as I found myself incapable of bearing it. Even during my surgical abortion procedure, I refused any sedation, other than local anesthesia; I wanted to be present in the only way in which I was capable. There are no words to describe the intense myriad of emotions that I went through, and I imagine that will help people understand why so few women are sharing their personal experiences of abortion here today. It's not that it's shameful; it's that it is the most singularly powerful, life-changing experience they've had, and to reduce that to three minutes of half-hearted listening would be crushing. I have made my peace with my decision, through enormous effort. Not only that, but I've worked on those other four factors. Thanks to Austin's Capitol Area Counseling, I have an amazing, an absolutely amazing and gifted counselor who is helping me reshape my concept of love, anger, and how to be true to myself. I've worked hard to get fit; I've gone from obese to healthy on the BMI scale in the last year. I believe were I faced with that choice now, that I could reach a different conclusion. Every step forward is a gift. It is empowering, and yet, it always has the lining of sadness, of loss, of the choice that I made. It will always be with me. It was the hardest choice I've ever had to make, and I don't wish it upon my worst enemy. Even if it made you understand, Mr. Chairman, that choosing abortion is not a choice against life, but a choice for life, I would not wish it upon you. I just ask you to keep in mind that number: that one in three women in our country have had or will have an abortion, and that it's not a choice made due to inconvenience, or a simplistic disregard of human life—quite the opposite. That when faced with a . . . with such a demanding, life-altering choice, most women will face a kaleidoscope range of emotions and thoughts that many humans will, if they are lucky, never have to face. As you can see, my choice had nothing to do with the availability of abortion. If abortion had been too expensive, or unavailable to me, I can promise you that I likely would have tried to create a cocktail of drugs to make it happen on my own. So, if a lack of available abortion providers is not a deterrent, what could you have done to prevent me from having an abortion? Perhaps working to remove the stigma of giving up unwanted pregnancies for adoption, perhaps making contraception more readily available via affordable healthcare, perhaps via that affordable healthcare providing quality counseling so that I had dealt with these issues much earlier in my life, or even so early that my parents could have had proper counseling and learned to deal with each other without so grossly perverting my concept of love and family. There are many ways in which to show that you value life without trying to force a choice in which you have neither responsibility nor consequences. I have to deal with my choice for the remainder of my life, and I will always work tirelessly to be a better person in the name of that choice. How are you going to work tirelessly to empower more women and families to rise to the occasion of unexpected pregnancy? Thank you for your time."

And now, members, I have personal testimonies that were sent to our office when people learned that we would be speaking against this bill today, and asked us to be their voice in this chamber.

This is from a young woman named Erica, and it's titled, "My Story":

"When I was young, I knew the older sister of a friend that was violently raped and was forced to bear the child. The young woman was a college student. One night, the rapist entered through her sliding glass door and raped her brutally, and left her battered. And as she healed, she discovered she was pregnant. Because abortions were illegal she had to suffer every day with the awful memories of that night, and she eventually dropped out of school. It was a nightmare for the entire family. When she walked down the street people would whisper about her being a rape victim. At the grocery store people would congratulate her and ask questions about her pregnancy, always reminding her that she was carrying the rapist's fetus. Rape can happen to anybody. As a mother I can not imagine forcing my child to endure that hell. The idea that the Texas government, my daughter can't decide with her doctor and family how to handle her most important decisions about her own body, sickens me. Thank you," and she signed it.

This is from Patricia, from Baylor, Texas:

"Dear Senator Davis, thank you with all my heart for standing up for all of us. It has been heartening to so many wonderful Texans fighting for Texas women these past few days. Your courage is particularly inspiring. It's way past time for Texas women to declare 'Don't tread on us', and mean it. In 1972 about 130,000 American women obtained illegal abortions or self-induced abortions. When I was in college one of my friends almost died of an illegal abortion; we aren't going back there. We cannot allow the extremist minority, propelled by ignorance, misogyny, hypocrisy, political showboating and the unconstitutional desire to impose their personal religious views on others, to control what women do with their own bodies. The hypocrisy is particularly brazen, the same fanatics who want to force women to bear babies they don't want and can't care for, lose all interest once the fetus is an actual born child. These are the same people who are trying to cut funding for food stamps, and further restrict Medicaid eligibility. Apparently they don't realize that once a child is born he needs food and basic medical care. And what about the libertarian mantra that we need to get government out of our lives, which somehow fails to apply when it comes to the most personal and private decision a woman may need to make. The government has no right to take my guns, but does have the right to force me to have a baby I can't care for? Please. I believe with all my heart that the real sin is not to have an abortion, but to bring into this world a child whom you know you cannot care for properly. We see the tragic consequences of that all around us: children abandoned, neglected, or mistreated, because they were never wanted or who had parents who were simply incapable of caring for them. I have three beautiful daughters; I want them to live happy, healthy lives, and to have children when the time is right for them. I want them to control their own destinies. Please keep fighting for them Wendy. With much gratitude and respect, Patricia."

From Ellen,

"Thank you so much for speaking for me and millions of other Texas women about the Republican attempts to dismantle women's healthcare. When I was seventeen I was raped on a date. I didn't know what had happened to me, let alone what to do when I wound up pregnant. My only thought was to kill myself, because I didn't know any other option available to me. Thankfully I had a smart, wonderful mother, who took me to have an abortion. The entire experience was horrible, but I cannot imagine what it would be like under the circumstance that Texas now wants to make women undergo. I made a decision to save a life, my own. And it was the most important decision I've ever made, and will ever make. Thank you Wendy for allowing me to tell my story, and continuing the fight."

From Patsy,

"Please be my voice. I have never needed an abortion but this should be the woman's choice. Sorry, God nor government got her pregnant, and therefore neither in my opinion enters into the decision. A woman's body is just that, her body. Therefore she should be able to decide on pregnancy issues. It's not that I believe in abortion, I would hope women would try to prevent a pregnancy before it happens. However, hormones being what they are, pregnancies happen and it should be the woman's right to decide if she wants to give birth. One hopes that there's a good guy involved who wants to be a good dad, but let's face it that's not always the case. Thank you for what you are about to do to speak up for women in Texas."

From Joyce,

"Would men want women to make the major choices about their lives and bodies for them? I don't think so. Why then do these Republican men think they are better qualified to make choices for women, than the women themselves are? Men say they want liberty, why then do they want to rob women of liberty? These men are acting and speaking out of arrogance, serving their own narrow and possessive self-interest. Do they really think women don't know this? It is time for men to shut up, and let women make their own choices about their own lives. Elizabeth Katie Stanton was right, everything that the King of England did to men during colonial times, the republican men and the Texas senate are doing to women now, and more. Signed, Joyce."

And this is from Dale,

"My story if of my first wife, who I met in my senior year at North Texas. She had a troubled childhood and was probably abused by an uncle and perhaps by her father. But for many years I did not know that. What I did know was a girl who was a talented writer and a passionate person. I was too young to know that she was troubled by things I could not then imagine. After graduation I took a job in Dallas and after a while she came to live with me. I think I wanted to marry her then but she did not want to commit to that. And after a year she left me and went to UT in Austin to study. For a while we were not communicating much, but we did write to let each other know where we were. She was going to classes, living in a house with a group of other students, and working in a clothing store in Hancock Center. That was forty years ago, and there was a lot of experimentation going on. She tried LSD and had flashbacks for years, and she probably had other drugs as well. At some point she was impregnated. I never knew whether she was raped or not, but I think that the odds are good that she was. By the time that happened we had been apart for over a year and I was living in Galveston. She came to me desperate with the story of what happened to her, and the confession that she had had an illegal and botched abortion done by a country doctor for $300. She went to work the next day and her fetus came out in a public restroom and was flushed down the toilet. When she got to Galveston she was ill and upset, and in a few days she was anemic from internal bleeding. I didn't understand what was happening, but got her to UT MD and she survived. The good thing was that it brought us back together, and I was able to care for her and marry her. I won't go into what happened next. But the point is, that in those days before safe and legal abortions, her story was not uncommon. And many girls who were not lucky died because of unsanitary or inept procedures. I don't know if this story will help you in your talking. A person who did not know Maryanne would write her off as a dissolute young woman who did drugs and had sex when she should not have, and perhaps not a good role model. But even then a civilized society should have treated her better. And when abortion became legal we thought that humanity had come with it. Maybe there is no way you can tell this story to the Senate, but I want you to understand what things were like then and what happened. And what happened to girls like her, and why we cannot let things go back to the way they were. Good luck and many thanks for your courage, Dale."

From Angela:

"I am fearful of raising my one and three year old girls in an environment where the government eliminates all but five clinics in the entire state, where women are allowed to make the most personal of decisions about their reproductive health. Where is all the paternalistic faux health and safety concern about vasectomies? Why should vasectomies be simple out-patient procedures when they pose such dire health risks to unsuspecting uneducated men? Doesn't such an invasive procedure mandate similar restrictions on clinics and doctors? For the health of men, of course. Angela."

This is from . . .

Lt. Gov. Dewhurst: Senator Deuell, for what purpose does the Senator from Hunt County wish to be recognized?

Senator Deuell: Mr. President, I was wondering if Senator Davis would answer some questions?

Dewhurst: Senator Davis, will you yield to Senator Deuell?

Davis: I'm happy to answer your question, Senator Deuell, but in doing so will not yield the floor . . . I do not give up the floor.

Dewhurst: You will maintain the floor for question, Senator Davis. Senator Deuell.

Deuell: Thank you, Mr. President. I have no intention of taking the floor from you, Senator Davis. I think all of us share the compassion for many of the people whose testimony you have read. I wanted . . . my first question is that some of the references that you've made and some of the references that some of the people whose testimony you read talk about women being degraded, called liars, or in some way being held in contempt. I was wondering what you found in this bill that holds any disregard for a woman facing the tough decision of whether or not to have an abortion?

Davis: What I find in this bill that disregards women who are confronting this decision are numerous. But I'll start with this, Senator Deuell: The ambulatory surgical center requirements have no basis in medical fact or science that necessitates the need for a woman to have an abortion procedure there, and in fact you will probably recall numerous times I asked Senator Hegar to provide some empirical evidence for us to understand what was unsafe in the clinical setting today, and how that would be made safer by virtue of this bill, and he was not able to provide any information to answer my question. That same question, I'm aware, was asked in the House hearings on this particular bill, and it was asked in the Senate hearings on this particular bill. And what we know, and I think we would agree, that today, of the 42 clinics that provide safe, legal abortion services for women in Texas, only 5 of those currently satisfy the conditions of the ambulatory surgical center. And I understand that the response has been given, "Make all the others come up," and there have been statements made that somehow abortion doctors are getting rich off of these facilities, and they ought to be willing to put this money back into them in order to assure that women have proper healthcare. But absent any justification, any reason that demonstrates why somehow these centers would provide better healthcare, I have to ask myself the question, and I know so many other women in Texas are asking themselves the question, "To what purpose, then, does this bill serve?" And could it be, might it just be a desire to limit women's access to safe, healthy, legal, constitutionally protected, abortions in the state of Texas?

Deuell: Well I know you've referenced a certain Twitter, but do you feel that that's the same sentiment by the members in this body who support this bill?

Davis: Senator Deuell, I don't want to impose upon any member an unkind starting point. I would hope to choose that every member on this floor shares a concern for women, men, and children. But because I've been unable to have a simple question answered that helps me understand how this leads to better care for women, I do have to question the justifying, the underlying reasons for advancing this.

Deuell: Why do you think the five clinics, the abortion clinics that have become ambulatory surgical centers, have done so?

Davis: You know, I don't have the expertise to answer that question.

Deuell: You don't think it might be to provide better care?

Davis: Well, you know what I think it might be is that years ago, before I was here in the Senate, a decision was made that for pregnancies of 16 weeks or longer, those needed to take place in ambulatory surgical centers. And I'm sure that there was some response to that in terms of the growth of these 5 centers in the state of Texas . . . to address that need. And I, as I said, was not here at that time, I don't know if there was information provided that because a . . . terminating a woman's pregnancy at 16 weeks or longer presented greater risk and that there actually was some connection made between that greater standard of medical facility and the ability to provide a safer environment for women existed. I don't know, but I would imagine that's why we have those 5.

Deuell: Well, do you remember the papers that I gave you about the requirements of an ambulatory surgical center some weeks ago when I spoke to the Democratic caucus?

Davis: Yes I do.

Deuell: Did you review that?

Davis: I browsed through it, yes; I didn't read it word for word.

Deuell: You compared it with . . . it's comparing with abortion centers and then the ambulatory surgical clinics. Why do we have . . . do you know why we have ambulatory surgical clinics, why we have that designation?

Davis: Well, my understanding is it's for procedures that might require a certain amount of medical attention that wouldn't otherwise be provided in another clinical setting. But I also understand, Dr. Deuell . . . Senator Deuell, that there are all sorts of outpatient procedures, some of which are more invasive than an abortion procedure, and we aren't requiring that they be delivered through the services of an ambulatory surgical center. And again, I'm yet to understand, I'm yet to hear that the specific reason is that this particular medical procedure should occur in such a facility, and I'm yet to understand how it is that we have not given pause to the impact that this will have on women's ability to access that safe, legal care. And when you layer it upon what happened in the last legislative session with the sonogram bill, I believe that in Texas a climate is being created that is slowly but surely chipping away at a woman's right to safe legal abortion . . . not because the right itself is being taken away, but because for some women the ability to access that right is being taken away.

Deuell: Well I don't agree that this bill does that, Senator Davis. The intent of this bill by the people that helped write it, and I'm one of them, is to increase safety. Now, you've cited evidence from ACOG and various other medical entities, but do you think that those entities who wrote you represent every physician in Texas?

Davis: Well of course they do not, and in fact I believe when I read through the letters from ACOG they describe themselves as a member organization, and I stated the number of doctors who are members of that organization, I can't remember what it was.

Deuell: Sure. Did you agree with ACOG's support of tort reform?

Davis: I do believe that tort reform was an important reform.

Deuell: So you agreed with them there. What . . . you've read a lot of testimony, are you going to read all of the testimony that was submitted at the committee meeting, both pro and con, or are you just reading testimony from people who are against this bill?

Davis: The testimony that I'm reading was from women who had signed up to speak and who, at the very late hour of about 1 A.M., were told they were not going to be able to.

Deuell: Sure, I understand that, but there were also people that were for this bill that didn't get to speak as well, is that not correct?

Davis: I'm sure that is correct, and I'm sure that you have the ability to read that information yourself if you'd like to read it and ask me a question about it.

Deuell: Well I don't have that available, I was just curious if you were gonna read everyone's testimony. Do you think the traditions of the Texas Senate are more important than women's safety?

Davis: Of course not.

Deuell: And you mentioned a raw abuse of power . . . could

you explain that a little bit? I mean, we have a process here, we . . . How do you feel that this bill is a raw abuse of power?

Davis: Well, first of all, I think it's a false choice to say that we should have to choose between women's health and the traditions of the Texas Senate. The traditions of the Texas Senate actually, in the regular session, assured that differing perspectives on women's health were made a part of the legislative decision making that occurred here. And, when I talk about abuse of power, I don't believe that in a little d Democratic state and individual should have the opportunity and the ability to override the expressed desires, thoughts, concerns, interests of people that are represented by the 31 senators here on the senate floor.

Deuell: Well, Senate Bill 5—

Davis: And, I believe—Let me finish answering you. And, I believe, that in the regular session, Democracy, the little d, worked to assure the balance of those opinions, made it's way into the bills that passed into law and those that did not.

Deuell: Well—

Davis: But! After we adjourned and, within the hour, as you know, we were called back by a single individual exercising his executive power over the state of Texas, Governor Perry. And you know, that another single individual and we've made our concerns known to our President about this, Lieutenant Governor Dewhurst, chose not to recognize the two-thirds rule as part of the way we would take up and consider legislation in the special session. I believe, that when two individuals exercise power in that way, it abuses the power they've been entrusted with, because it denies the minority voices who are represented by Democratic senators on this floor an opportunity to be heard.

Deuell: Well, thank you. [*Applause.*]

Dewhurst: Other senators did mention me by name. Please, if you can, maintain decorum.

Deuell: Well, Senator Davis, Senate Bill 537, which was the

facilities bill which was my bill in the regular session, had 20 senators supporting it. That's 61.3 percent of the senate so, when you speak of minorities and minority rule and raw power, do you not think it's fair that when 60 percent of the senators want that bill to be passed, that perhaps, it's fair that it should since it probably represents a majority of the people of Texas?

Davis: Well, the polling doesn't demonstrate that it represents the majority of the people in Texas and, of course, you know as well as I do, and we can have a very long conversation, Senator Deuell, about the consequences of a history of redistricting in the state of Texas.

Deuell: Well, I understand that, but my particular district—the last time I ran against a Democrat, I got 67 percent of the vote, and I've been unapologetic about being pro-life. So, would you certainly not think, then, that my vote to be pro-life and my support of this bill would represent the majority, the overwhelming majority, of my district and then that, perhaps, it's also true to the other senators supporting this bill?

Davis: I think that very well may be the case, Senator Deuell, but I also think that many people in your district may have voted for you for other reasons than that and, in fact, often times on both sides of the party isle, people vote based on the letter that's next to your name on the ballot. And, it doesn't necessarily reflect their individual independent decisions on a variety of issues, then it may be the case that they feel on balance you represent their perspectives on most issues. But, I would imagine, there are probably people who voted for you and people who voted for some of the other Republican senators who are on our floor today, who disagree with taking a decision on these particular bills, even if they themselves identify as Republicans and typically voted Republican.

Deuell: Do you think you have constituents that voted for you that are in support of this bill?

Davis: That's probably likely.

Deuell: Another question I wanted to ask Senator was, I think it was your words, that this was treating women as though they're not capable. I think for most women who choose to have an abortion it's the first time, although that's not always the case. But, you know, women, as you've pointed out by some of the testimony who are facing this tough decision, are very vulnerable. Do you, given what's happened in Philadelphia and Houston and some other abortion clinics in these squalid conditions, do you think, perhaps, that some of these vulnerable women should not have the state of Texas protect them by setting standards of care for their abortion?

Davis: I think that the state of Texas has already established a fine standard of care. In fact, I've sighted that from one of the letters that I read. A woman who works at one of these facilities talked about the variety of state agencies and uh municipal agencies that regulate them. And, I think that we are doing our job, certainly with the passage of constitutional protections for women, and their ability to choose, to make such a difficult decision. We've seen the standard of care rise tremendously, because women are able to go to legal facilities that provide safe care for them.

Deuell: And you think all abortion facilities are adequate for these women?

Davis: Senator Deuell, I'm sure just like every other clinic that treats colds, that treats geriatrics, perhaps dentist offices, orthodontists, I can't stand here today and tell you that every single one of them provides good care. But, what I can tell you is, that they have regulations in place that require that they do, and that we have the ability to respond when they don't. And, again, where this particular bill is concerned, no one has said anything about the existing requirements in these facilities that is somehow creating an endangered environment for women. I have no doubt, that in one, or two, or some of them, one or two or some women may have experienced care that none of us would be happy with. But, it isn't because the facility was the problem, and it wasn't because the standards in the facility were a problem, and it wasn't because the regulations of those facilities were a problem, it's because sometimes, when human beings are involved, as you know in providing care, sometimes that care is what we all wished it would be. And, changing to an ambulatory surgical center, is going to do nothing to address that.

Deuell: Well, I would disagree. I think that, if you look at the regulations and the scrutiny and, if you might want to go back and review this paper that I gave you, you would see that perhaps it would insure that every woman gets a safe abortion under the best possible care. You know, Senator Davis, this bill really is about women's health. It really is about abortions. Mr. President, I don't remember the opposition, or our side making any snide comments as Senator Davis spoke, and I would appreciate you holding decorum in this hall to the same standard. Mr. President—

Davis: I've not yielded the floor—

Senator Williams: Pardon me. Mr. President, can you describe, for the body and our guests, rule 306 and what the punishment for obstruction of proceedings here in the Senate is?

[*mumbled voices, shuffling in room*]

Dewhurst: You're asking me to read, to read the rule?

Williams: I-I-I'm asking, if, yeah, I think that maybe we need to remind her about what the enforcement mechanism under rule 306 is for this.

Dewhurst: I'm sure everyone here is going to make best efforts to have umm, good, very good decorum but our rule 306 does say, "The Senate during its sessions may imprison for 48 hours any person not a member for violation of the Senate rules, for disrespectful and disorderly conduct in its presence, or for obstructing any Senate, uh, proceeding."

Williams: Thank you, Mr. President.

Dewhurst: I'm sure everyone is going to behave themselves.

Deuell: Thank you, Mr. President. Senator Davis are, are you taking the position that if this bill becomes law and every abortion clinic in Texas becomes an ambulatory, surgical center that women would not be safer and get better care?

Davis: No, I'm taking the position that if this bill becomes law not every ambul-, not every facility will have the capacity and the resources to become an ambulatory, surgical center and that women who currently are being provided care, very safe care, in existing clinics today will be denied that access. Because they want—

Deuell: Why do you think that clinics will close? I mean, that's been, there's 5 clinics that are ambulatory surgical centers and there's, I guess, three dozen or so other clinics and what I've heard throughout this debate is that all of those clinics would close, but why do you think they would close?

Davis: Well, Senator Deuell, because it's incredibly expensive to bring them up to this, uhh, requirement and in some of them, quite physically, quite, quite literally. Physically, it would be impossible it would require the closure and probably the from the ground up new building of an ambulatory/surgical center at great cost and, an, and the concern and the point that I have about that is, we aren't doing that in any other arena of healthcare. We aren't saying that a vasectomy has to take place there. We aren't saying that a colonoscopy has to take place there. We aren't saying that a live birth has to take place in such a setting and what I'm suggesting is when we're demonstrating that we're going to put restrictions in place, rules in places, standards in place that are going to dramatically increase the cost of delivering that care, I do not doubt for a moment that there are some of those clinics who simply aren't going to have the financial capacities to accommodate that and, not only do I not doubt that for a moment but, what I fear most is that in the areas of our state that are most impoverished that those will be the most likely areas where these will not produce. Where these will not have the resources to appear and where women who, again, layered upon the sonogram from last session, who now have to have a sonogram, a 24-hour waiting period, return, make sure the same doctor who did the sonogram is the person who performs her abortion and if, for some reason, that doctor can't be there the next day, she's gotta start the whole process over again. I'm worried that women that are already going through that an, an, and it's so easy for us to disregard as we stand here in our nice clothing, in our relatively comfortable lives, it's so easy for us to say, "Why is that a big deal?" Senator Deuell, it's a big deal. It is a big deal and I have been there. That has been my life. I have been to the point when I literally could not put gasoline in my car to go anywhere but from work and back because I could not afford an extra gallon of gas to make any other trips. And these are the women who are impacted by these kinds of decisions and shouldn't we be able to say to them that there is a reason for it. That there is absolute health reasons for it. And if there isn't, shouldn't we all agree that making sure that they have access is the best thing that we can do for their healthcare and their—

Deuell: Senator Davis, the medical literature supports that the higher standards a given surgical center has the better outcomes and all women have. You stated that the legislature has never before dictated such requirements. I could run you through my medical office in Greenville. Oh and, by the way, I take care of a lot of low income women and I have, I was at the federally qualified health clinic for there. I take a lot of Medicaid patients. I understand. I've given patients gas money before so that they could get home aft, after they saw me. But, if you look at every clinic and you look at what's required for a family medicine clinic or a pediatric clinic of a federally qualified health clinic, government dictates safety factors all of the time. We have to have people come through and look at our ophthalmoscopes and our otoscopes and put a sticker on them every year when there's very little, uh, chance for them t, to malfunction. We have to have a crash cart, I mean, I could go on and on and on, it is not unprecedented for the state, uh, or the federal government to require these requirements. And, in an abortion, even in the first trimester there are complications that can occur that can be devastating and even life threatening. A uterus has a blood flow of 500cc's a minute and sometimes, even under good hands, bad things can happen. And that's what we're trying to do. The medication with the RU486, bad things can happen. I want to quote a journal here. You've quoted, uhh, some authorities. This is a, uh, entitled "Immediate Complications After Medical Compared with Surgical Termination of Pregnancy" and it's been cited that the complication rate is 0.5% different. This study showed, uh, it said the overall incidence of adverse effects was fourfold higher in the medical compared with surgical abortion cohort. Twenty percent with medical abortions versus 5.6. And this was published in *Obstetrics and Gynecology* in 2009. My point is, that perhaps, an abortion performed in a surgical center, perhaps all that they would have is not needed. But what about that one woman that does need it and that one life that's saved, it's already been through a lot of tragedy to make this. I mean, do you not see that this bill will provide the safest care for a woman who decides to have an abortion?

Davis: Senator Deuell, first of all, I want to say that I, I respect you so much, I truly do. You are a good person. You are a good doctor. You are a good senator. And I know you care about people and I do not intended to suggest that you do not. But we have a difference of opinion. I believe that a nexus should be shown between the need to move to this sort of a standard of care and truly ensuring a better outcome for women's health. I believe that that nexus has not been demonstrated here and I understand your point that if an argument could be made that even one woman would be made safer by virtue of it doesn't it make sense. But I would ask you to consider, th, the very valid concern that there are many women who will lose their access to care as a consequence of this law. And that one woman or that 20 women or that 300 women or that 3,000 women should cause you and me and everyone else on this floor great concern.

Deuell: Well that's a big disagreement we have also because I honestly don't see any reason for any of these clinics to close. Th, th, they make a lot of money with these abortions. Look at, you saw the list of surgical clinics in the state of Texas, 400 and some of them and many of them are in smaller towns, than the smallest area of an abortion clinic, and we've exempted abortion clinics that do 50 or less procedures. Uhh so, again, I go back to, you know, I, we, I will not concede that any of these clinics have to close. So, I'm just, you know, we could maybe stop at this point and disagree, umm, but I do not believe any of them have to close. I believe the money is there and I believe for the safety of women that they should do so. That's really what this debate is about. And I appreciate you too. Obviously, you wouldn't go through what you're going through now if you didn't believe, um, believe in it. But, uhh, I'd like to go on, I have some more questions in other areas. Uhh, uhh I wanted, I wanted to ask you . . . when you were talking about the 20 weeks, and there was some questions and some of the testimony about gestational age and I believe ACOG mentioned about the last menstrual period and how we figure that . . .

Davis: Yeah.

Deuell: and in the bill it references actual fertilization and I don't think that matters as long as we all know what we're talking about. But you said that there, um that there was nothing in this bill that allowed for extenuating circumstances, but on page 5, line 21, and I'll read it to you and I don't want to, mean to be condescending. I just happen to have it and maybe you don't, but it says, "The prohibitions and requirements under sections 171.043, 171.044, and 171.045, they do not apply to an abortion performed on an unborn child who has severe fetal abnormalities,." It seems to me that that would take care of situations that you described where, uh, perhaps the parents, didn't find out until after the 20-week period. So, um, I wanted to clarify that or at least get your comments on that part.

Davis: Well, I appreciate the clarification and I think that some of that testimony that I read had occurred prior to the substitute language. Um, Senator I think the language previously, uh, that was cited by ACOG and some of the other expert testimony which I, uh, I think really created the reason for the change in the language, necessitated that change, and, um, and put it in the terms that you just read. I think some of the lingering questions though from ACOG, was what that would mean and their responsibility as doctors, uh, to make this determination in terms of what that means and whether there might be some liability or greater exposure on their part, having to make that particular decision.

Deuell: Ok. Thank you. Then um I wanted to address the physician privilege, you know, as a licensed physician in Texas, I am required by the medical practice act, in fact, the Texas Board of Medicine oversees that. I'm required to provide for follow-up care, after-hours care of my patients. Fortunately, I have nine very understanding partners who cover for me when I am down here. But it, uh, what I have, uh, heard from patients who have had abortions and then had complications and then end up in Greenvilles is that they called the clinic that they had the abortion and they couldn't reach anyone and do you not think that a physician who performs an abortion should be responsible for the after-care, especially for immediate complications of an abortion?

Davis: I believe, and I think, most women in Texas would agree that it would make very good sense that women who had such a procedure, any procedure. I've had my wisdom teeth taken out and my dentist has provided me his phone number, uh, if I have any concerns in the night, with 24-hour ability to call and, uh, let him or her know that I had a problem arise. I don't think that anyone would disagree that those sorts of regulations provide a better climate. If they don't already exist in abortion clinics, in the state of Texas, and I don't think that's what the disagreement for this particular bill is.

Deuell: Well, one thing that was mentioned, um, I wanted to clarify that you said about the Texas Hospital Association. No hospital is required to grant privileges to a doctor, is that not true?

Davis: That's absolutely true and, uh, I think that that's part of the concern because where we require in law that a, an abortion provider, be granted admitting privileges, the fact of the matter is, hospitals across the state, exercise their own decision-making with regards to whether they grant those admitting privileges and, and, what it would mean if fewer doctors who would have the ability to perform abortions in Texas. So, it's sort of the double whammy. The double whammy of having to have an ambulatory surgical center which, there will now be fewer abortion centers in the state of Texas. You and I will disagree over that. But then having fewer doctors who are qualified and able to give that care, and, and, when we talked about this bill in the regular session, I asked Senator Hagar, about that woman who lives in Laredo who if she shows up at the emergency room in Laredo, obviously, that hospital is going to have the ability to provide care to her. I think it makes sense that they would be able to contact a doctor who has performed an abortion on her and ask questions if the need be. But I don't see any connection to providing better healthcare to the woman if she had an abortion all the way in San Antonio because it was the only clinic available to her. And the fact that the, the person who performed that doesn't have admitting privileges at a hospital near to her.

Deuell: Do we have any data about how far women have to travel to get an abortion? Are they . . . since there are abortion centers in most every, the, the major cities. Do we know how many women have to travel those long distances?

Davis: Well, under this bill, uh, right now because only 5 centers would still be open we know women would have to travel hundreds of miles. But when we debated the sonogram bill, I clearly remember, although I can't cite to you the specifics, Senator Uresti, making the very legitimate points about indeed how far women have to travel. And in fact, that's why an exception was made to the 24-hour waiting period between the sonogram and the procedure for certain areas of our state, because there are such long distances women have to travel.

Deuell: When a hospital grants hospital privileges they require a certain amount of training and ability by the physician. Is there concern that perhaps the physicians doing abortions wouldn't have the credentials to be privileged by a hospital in 30-mile range?

Davis: I'm sorry, can you repeat the question?

Deuell: Hospitals set standards for getting privileges.

Davis: Yes.

Deuell: You know, when I apply and reapply to the hospital that I practice at both here and in Greenville, they look at my medical school, they look at my residency, they look at my continuing medical education, they look at whether I'm board certified. There's a certain standard that a physician has to make to get hospital privileges. Is there a concern that the doctors performing abortions would not meet the criteria to get privileges at these various hospitals?

Davis: Well, I think that under the letter that we heard from the Texas Hospital Association, there may be indeed that problem. Where the hospital may not, for whatever their reasons are, want to grant privileges to that particular doctor. They grant privileges to the doctors whose expertise they need, and if they've filled that need it's not at all atypical that hospitals choose not to simply go with an unlimited number of doctors allowing them admitting privileges. So, it may be the case that doctors that are perfectly capable, um, wonderful, uh, tremendously well-educated and good doctors don't get admitting privileges to a hospital simply because the expertise that they have is not something that the hospital needs.

Deuell: Well, but the doctors performing abortions would have to have certain training credentials. Do you think it's good to have abortions done by doctors who couldn't get basic hospital privileges?

Davis: But that's not why—you're assuming that the reason they wouldn't get the basic hospital privileges is because they don't have somehow adequate training or credentials in order to get it. And we know, again, based on what THA is saying to us, that there are multiple reasons why hospitals don't grant admitting privileges to doctors.

Deuell: Well, now, my point is that the angst about this part of the bill would be that many of these doctors would not have the credentials to be given admitting privileges to a hospital. And that perhaps this also is a safety, uh, part of the bill. But I'd like to go on, if we can. You've mentioned about the health of the mother and you've mentioned that the mother would have—pregnant woman would have to be brought to the point of compromise of immediate injury or death. And yet I can't really see that in the bill. Uh, would you explain how the bill would prevent a woman who chooses to have an abortion or the doctors, uh, having to wait until there's an immediate danger, as opposed to, uh, a danger that could be caught a little earlier?

Davis: Well, in the bill, and— I'm going to have to find the page. Hang on, I'm trying to mark my spot here. In the bill it speaks to—

Deuell: I would—page 2, line 2b, uh, might address that, Senator. If you want to start there we could go through it. Oh that's . . . Sorry that was my mistake. My point is that I don't see that in there. Page 5 line 1 it does not apply to an abortion performed if there exists a condition that in the physician's reasonable medical judgment—we're giving the judgment to the physician; we're not dictating I might add—so complicates the medical condition of the woman that to revert the woman's death or a serious risk of substantial and irreversible physical impairment of a major bodily function, other than a psychological condition it necessitates as applicable and then it lists one, two, and three. I don't see how that forces a position to wait until the woman is in immediate danger. Number one it talks about the immediate abortion if her pregnancy without the delay is necessary to determine. We're talking about not dating the baby if there's a situation, in other words they don't have to worry what about what the gestational date is. And then two, the abortion of a pregnancy, even though the post-fertilization age of the unborn child is 20 or more weeks, that tells me that if there is a condition that threatens the life of the mother, that you don't have to wait until that's about to happen. It can be done as long as they believe that it's going to happen. I don't see where you came to the conclusion that they would have to wait.

Davis: Senator I was reading from the testimony that someone provided. What I recall though from the information that we received, concerns that we received from doctors, I think this is something that we received from ACOG. I'm not sure if it's the testimony that I read to the record, but they talk very specifically about exempting physicians where the procedure could be authorized if there was risk of death or substantial irreversible physical impairment of a major bodily function. I think the concern that they were raising as I recall it, was putting a doctor into that decision-making role, and that where a doctor has to make that judgment call in some instances they may not make it. They may instead force a woman or refuse to provide a service to a woman out of fear that somehow that broad category is going to arise and the concern was really more one of the liability and increased liability of doctors, because of this particular provision than it was the immediacy of them making the decision.

Deuell: Since I'm not an obstetrician gynecologist, and I had concerns, but I just want to point out now that it says very clearly it does, says requirements under these sections do not apply to an abortion and it lists those areas. And again I realize you are reading testimony and some of that testimony if not a lot of it was more anecdotal than expert, but doctors are protected under this and there is provisions as I pointed out earlier for fetal abnormality. Um, Senator Davis, um, the 1973 Roe v. Wade, the supreme court said that abortions could be allowed up to the point of viability. As I pointed out in my floor testimony earlier, uh, things have changed a lot. Are you aware that there are a lot of babies being aborted in Texas that are way past the viability age uh, for no other reason than, uh, it's not wanted.

Davis: Than what, Senator?

Deuell: The baby is not wanted, there's no medical issue, it's passed the age of viability, that there are abortions occurring in Texas that are running into the third trimester.

Davis: In fact the information, the empirical information that I've read suggests, that only I think .5 or 6 percent of abortions are ever performed passed that 20-week period. It might have been up to 1 percent. I'm sorry I can't quite trust my memory on that, but in that instance, a very low instance rate where post 20-week abortions occur, most of those are situations where a mother's life was in jeopardy or there were very severe problems with the fetus. I don't think it's the case that women are just waiting for their third trimester and suddenly decide now is the time to show up to get an abortion.

Deuell: Well I would submit that it's probably not the greater number of abortions, but uh you know dating a pregnancy is hard. Um, it's last menstrual period, it's active intercourse, it's physical exam, it's a sonogram, there's a blood test you can do called a quantitative beta hcg and all of those sometimes don't add up and my point in bringing this up in terms of the 20-week part of this bill and in terms of the regulation of medical abortions and having all abortions centers be ambulatory surgical clinics is that sometimes mistakes are made and they are well intentioned in the sense that good doctors are just trying to get the right dates and the date is not always accurate and I would just make the point again about these ambulatory surgical centers, sometimes a baby is small for gestational age, it's further along, there's questions about dates and all that adds up and sometimes bad things can happen with the dates and that again is another reason that we support having all the centers be an ambulatory surgical clinic. Senator Davis I don't have any other questions at this time, I appreciate your answers and I'm glad that we could have a civil discussion here on the floor. Thank you so much for answering my questions.

Davis: As am I Senator Deuell, thank you for your, for your questions.

Senator Eddie Lucio: Mr. President.

Dewhurst: Mr. Lucio for what purpose?

Lucio: Will Senator Davis yield?

Davis: I will be happy to yield to you Senator Lucio but I do not give up the floor.

Lucio: I appreciate the tone of the conversation that just took place between Senator Deuell. I want to have the same type of conversation, one that's sincere. I know that you speak from your heart and I do too. You well know that I have a great deal of respect for everything you said about the respect you have for Senator Deuell, I have for you and more. I think we know that. I did just want to take in a very nice way an issue that the first thing you said in your opening remarks when you said that and you set up the categories—two categories of legislators who are either or supporting this bill, you said partisan partisanship, which I don't fall under.

Davis: No you do not.

Lucio: I'm a democratic pro-life legislator, and then lacking the strength to oppose it. And I know that on the contrary you do know that I do have an inner strength that supports this bill and that strength is in the name of my faith as a Roman Catholic. I um really also took issue with one of the letters that you read that said that some of us were showboating because of our religious beliefs and I take issue with that because that's never been the case with this legislator anyway and I take it to heart. Everything I do and when I've joined with you and others in supporting funding for healthcare and it's pained me and it's hurt me deeply two sessions ago, last session, when we cut healthcare by 7.2 billion dollars, in this state. And education by 5.4, however, the reason we stand here today is because I made a decision to honor a calling . . .

Davis: Yea

Lucio: And I voted against suspension yesterday.

Davis: Yes.

Lucio: And I did because it was the right thing to do, it was the Christian thing to do in my belief, because our colleague had lost her grandchild and her father and was tied up with family to be able to, to um, get by the day, uh, with so much hurt. And I joined with her last night and I paid my respects on behalf of the entire senate and staff. So I decided to go ahead and allow this to start today. One vote. That's how powerful a senate vote is sometimes—one, one legislator, one vote can change the way things happen. And I wish you well physically and mentally because I know that you have a big resolve in what you believe and you're going to take this to the midnight hour and kill this bill. I feel awful about that for various reasons because I know there's so many abortions going on on a daily basis in this state and this country. Um, senator, are you aware of how many abortions have taken place since *Roe v. Wade* started in 1973, up to date?

Davis: Senator, you gave us a piece of paper on the floor the other day that had that number, but I, I don't recall it. You'll have to refresh my memory.

Lucio: Well, for those that are here, and not aware, there's been 56—56 million, 353 thousand, 184. Now statistics that are internet show today there was 2,206 abortions so far in the United States. This year, 581 thousand, 166 thousand in the Unites States. By Planned Parenthood 163,969, and due to rape and incest 5,637. My heart really hurts when I hear those two words, rape and incest. You know I love women because, um, I have fond memories of my grandmothers, my Mama, who I thank for life. I'm one of ten kids, as you well know, so we were reared being pro-life. We even adopted a sister because she was dying and my Dad had the heart of gold, brought her home, and we, she's 61-years-old now, brought home at four months, she was four months old. So, to me, it's easy to stand before this body, or anywhere in public and talk about the sanctity of life and the importance there is for us to be thankful about life. The letters that you wrote were heartfelt, and I cried inside when you were crying because of the hardships that women face in this world. But I also thought about the 56 million plus babies that would never be born, would never be able to write a letter to their legislators talking about how they felt about life and how grateful they might have been, you know, for their mothers to be giving them that opportunity. The point I want to make is that the majority, the majority of abortions that are being conducted are in this state and country are as the result of unwanted pregnancies and that, that is hard for me to understand, because there's so many out there that I also run into who want to adopt someone, they want a baby, they can't have babies, and yet we haven't talked one minute on this floor or in committee about the rights of the unborn. No one's talked about the rights of the unborn. They don't have any, quite frankly, because of *Roe v. Wade*. And it pains me to know, because of my religious belief, that we'll continue because of the deaths of this bill, continue to see more death. I talked about a culture of death and why shouldn't I talk about that when I see the statistics before me that are true. And it pains me just to know that more will die during this debate right now. And if the governor doesn't call for another special session, well we won't have an opportunity to address this issue, then more will die. I share with you, I, I, I, agree with you and I share your thoughts about helping women find the necessary healthcare services they deserve, other than abortion. And I make that very clear for today. I will continue, and my record speaks for itself, to vote—and I even supported Planned Parenthood, for them to be funded on everything other than anything that lead to abortions. Because I will continue to fight for the unborn, I will continue to speak for them, because they can't speak for themselves, they can't, they will never have an opportunity to sit down and write me a letter, or you a letter, or anyone a letter, or in a school house, or grow up and have their own babies. So I, I just needed to make that statement while those that are here today listen on. And I urge everyone to go home and write their mamas a letter and thank them for being pro-life or else they wouldn't be here today. I wouldn't be here today. I think those that got here today are very fortunate to have a mom or a dad or either one that thought it necessary for them to live, so that they too could enjoy life, as God would want us to. And I thank you for this heartfelt conversation because I have a great deal of respect for you.

Davis: Senator Lucio, you are one of my dearest friends in the Senate Chamber and I believe you have a compassionate heart beyond compare, and as I read some of those letters that folks have written to us on this particular issue and they've called upon us to be pro-life in all regards if we're going to be pro-life, um, and I would suggest that you are the template that exhibits that. Not only do you stand very firmly based on your faith, and I know it is a deep faith; I see you every day reading your Bible on your iPad as you sit here on the senate floor. I know that your decision on these issues comes from that very deep place of faith. I also know that you are a man who fights for children in need. I watched you this session work on the food bill, and I watched how hard it was for you, and I, I saw the sadness and the despair that you had, day after day, as you tried to convince a two-thirds majority of the Senate to suspend, so that your bill to feed hungry children in schools could pass. In all respects, you've demonstrated a care and concern after a child is born, before so, and you are consistent beyond compare and I respect you tremendously. I'm sorry that we disagree on this particular issue. I think that, by your very comments, though, clearly your understanding, your hope for what this bill would achieve is that abortion services would decrease in Texas. Um, I don't think that that's been the stated purpose for this bill. It's been stated that it's to make women who are having an abortion safer and provided better healthcare. But I appreciate your candor, I appreciate your support, the incredible good work that organizations like Planned Parenthood do to try to get that number down, that very alarming number you read. I don't think that there's a person on this floor who would say that we should feel good about that. And I know that you've supported making sure that women have access to family planning and healthcare services which I believe is the number one way we'll get that number down and I thank you for your support on those issues.

Lucio: Thank you Senator Davis. I just, you know, 56.3 million is two times the population of Texas and growing; let's continue to find the funding necessary for children with special needs, women with everyday needs, but let's also try and find a way of ending abortion. I just feel that we have neglected the rights of the unborn at this point in Texas, and I hope that we can take a good turn, to the right or left, but not go down the path that we've been on for so long. Thank you.

Davis: Thank you Senator.

Lucio: Thank you Mr. President.

President: Senator Davis you have the floor.

Davis: Thank you. I'll continue reading these letters. I don't have too too many more of them. This one is from someone named Raul:

"Senator I have four adult daughters, and I appreciate you standing up for the right to choose what to do with their bodies and to continue to have that option. I would never encourage my daughter to have an abortion. However I believe in my heart that they must have the choice available to them. Let's keep our State moving forward and not regress to a time where women had to take huge health risks on top of the weight of a very personal situation. Keep up the fight and I will pray (yes, a Christian praying for you) may God give you the strength to prevail in your effort to stand up. Not only to defend women but the laws of our great country."

This is from a person named Nancy. Nancy writes:

"Last year when they passed the sonogram law I was so upset I actually sent an email message to Governor Perry's office to veto the measure. I'm pretty sure he never saw it but I had to express my dismay. You and I know it takes two people to conceive a baby, but if the pregnancy is unexpected or poorly timed, and the male partner leaves the relationship, the female bears the total physical, emotional, economic, and social obligation to raise the child. She has a few choices and if she is lucky she will have family to help her with support if necessary. To conceive a child for many women is easy. To raise a child is really hard. To give birth and then place that child up for adoption is excruciating. To decide to abort is a truly hard decision, not made lightly, and forever remembered. These are forever decisions. Why do men think they have the right to decide this very personal decision of a woman? To have no options except a backroom, unsafe, and unsanitary procedure puts women back into the 19th century. It's obvious that the governor and the Republicans of Texas care very little for the health of the women of this state. They also do not care for the quality of life for the children of this state. Unwanted children often suffer malnutrition, poor early development, abuse, neglect, and have lower self-esteem. A child should be born into a loving environment where it can grow and develop into a productive adult. Since the educational system of Texas now spends at the level less than 48 other states on the public education for the children in the state, it would seem that the state might want fewer children encumbered with a lack of nutrition, early childhood development, and social skills. By making abortions more difficult to obtain, more children will be born in Texas to families who cannot provide for them, or to single mothers without resources to create a nurturing environment. Women will go to other states, backrooms, or illegal centers. There might also be an increase in abuse to women because they got pregnant. It is amazing that men make the laws that regulate women's bodies. If men carried babies, went through childbirth, and survived the continual responsibility for more than 18 years required to raise a child, they may think differently. They are removed from a good portion of child-care, even if they think they are being proactive parents. Whether I believe in or would seek an abortion is not the issue. It is whether the option is available to a woman who would seek an abortion. It is extremely personal. To formulate legislation so that option is no longer available removes a woman's rights to control her own body. That legislation does not change the morality of anyone. It only increases the anguish some women must go through. I would never require anyone to have an abortion, but should I encounter someone who does want the procedure, than I want it readily available. There are many reasons a woman may want to abort: drug consumption during pregnancy, failed contraceptive, casual sexual encounter, economic strain on the current family, too young, known deformed fetus, and probably many others I cannot list. In the right situation these are all viable reasons to not continue a pregnancy. Thank you for trying to stop this regressive and damaging legislation, Nancy."

This is from Paul. He writes:

"In Judaism, the health of the mother is paramount. The fetus is considered part of the mother's body, not a person with preferential rights. In Exodus 21, verse 22, when a miscarriage results from a woman injured as a bystander to a fight, the guilty party must compensate the woman (her husband, actually, but this was 3,300 years ago) just as they would be compensated for the loss of an arm. Therefore if carrying the baby to term would seriously threaten the mother's health, abortion is not just permissible, it is required in the same manner as the removal of a severely affected or damaged extremity. This legislation would take an alternative religious view—that the fetus is a separate, full person whose rights are superior to those of the mother, and imposing it in those who hold a different, sincerely held religious belief in absolute violation of both U.S. and Texas constitutions. Just as it would be impermissible to require the Jewish standard to be imposed on the devout Catholics or Baptists, who believe that separate life begins at conception, and the fetus take precedence over the health of the mother, it is equally wrong to impose a standard that violates the Jewish and biblical principle of the primacy of the mother on someone who observes that understanding. I hope this helps to inform and fill some of the many hours you have ahead, Paul."

From Penny:

"My mom died three years ago at 92. With three small children and a husband war-wounded in WWII, she was in psychical danger from an unexpected, forced pregnancy. Abortions were legal in the 1940's and one, although sad, saved her life and our family. How could these people who want to prevent all abortions have looked into our eyes, ages five, three, and two, and said: 'It was for the greater good for our mother to die when she could be, and was, saved'? Penny."

From Sharon:

"I stand for you as you battle for women's rights in Texas. I am a born-and-bread Catholic Texan with two daughters and one granddaughter. To think that my children's rights could be trampled by this bill simply enrages me. We have been so very blessed thus far with healthy and planned pregnancies. But that could change in the blink of an eye. No one ever foresees the crisis of the magnitude and despair that many women face. I fully support your efforts to stop this bad bill. I am pro-life and pro-choice. I also teach, so I look into the eyes of poverty each and every class day. I believe that as new Texans are born, their needs should be taken care of, but I don't see that happening. Shutting down clinics for women's health is certainly a giant leap in the wrong direction. Surely our esteemed legislators are all well aware of the good that places like Planned Parenthood do. They prevent so many pregnancies as well as assist pregnant women to find adoptive loving homes for babies. Yet it is so very obvious that this bill is a purely political bill designed to attract certain voters. Well, there are many other voters out here in this great big state, voters who want Texas to move forward not backward. I stand united with you, Senator Davis, and the countless other women who have fought for the rights of women. This is 2013; what a travesty that in this new century so many in our Texas legislature want to reverse the progress women, and men, have made."

This from Myrtle:

"In 1944 when I was 10 years old, I almost lost my mother from a botched abortion. For the first time in many years financially she was making it, but she knew that my grandmother, who had taken care of me and my sister, could no longer care for an infant, so she went to my dad's cousin, her obstetrician, and he refused to do it as he could lose his license. Instead she went to the neighborhood abortionist. Afterwards she started to bleed profusely. My dad called his cousin who again refused to treat my mother. Dad finally found a doctor willing to keep my mother from bleeding to death. It was months 'til she felt well again. She suffered from severe anemia and severe depression. Mother started speaking out for legalized abortion when Roe v. Wade came about. She didn't want any other woman to suffer like she did. Fortunately no one else in my family has had to face the challenge of an unwanted pregnancy. I've spent 8 years as a volunteer going through labor with women at John Peter Smith hospital. There they do not do abortions, they also do not train doctors to do them. Where is a poor woman in Tarrant County going to go if the proposed law passes?"

And this is from Judy:

"As a divorcée of 75 with four happily married children, I don't personally have a dog in this fight, but I am horrified for the women and children who will go without medical care because clinics are closed. Many women will die of female diseases, but the old angry white men don't care. I don't understand how they can turn their backs on women's health needs. Needs of which they have no understanding or knowledge. I read some of them don't even know what a rape kit is. Let them be told vasectomies are against the law and listen to the uproar. I grew up as a doctor's daughter in the days of back-alley coat-hanger abortions. And I remember too well a frantic call from a surgeon to my dad. I told him my dad was sleeping and he swore and said he didn't care. To get him now. The surgeon had been called to help another doctor with a patient and when he got there he discovered it was an illegal abortion. The patient died. The surgeon who had not participated saw his career go down the tubes and needed my dad's advice. I remember too, always, my friend whose college roommate died from an illegal abortion. We can't possibly go back to those days. If one of my daughters or daughters-in-law wanted an abortion, I would be heartbroken, but it would be their choice. Not a decision made by me or by men in a legislature."

This is from Edie. Edie writes:

"First thank you for your courage in standing for Texas women. We need a lot more legislators in our Texas Legislature like you. We all know this bill has nothing to do with protecting women's health, in fact, it will do the opposite. I'm amazed that Republicans think this will win them elections. Primaries maybe, but not elections. The truth is that women will always need and get abortions. I am old enough to remember when abortions were not legal. I remember girls that were sent away who had babies that they were too young to care for and giving them up for adoption, not even understanding what they were signing or it's significance. I remember a college friend having a back-alley abortion. Fortunately she was okay, but it was very expensive and she had to drop out of school for a semester. I know another young woman who got pregnant at 26 by a man who was just a boyfriend. She was lucky that the Supreme Court had just made abortion legal and she was able to get one in a hospital and avoid an unwanted pregnancy with a man she did not plan to spend her life with. Somehow the right-to-lifers are happy to protect the fetuses of the unborn but care nothing for the women who would be giving birth to the fetus. She seems to have no rights, even in cases of rape or incest. Once a child is born the right-to-lifers move on to the next pregnant woman to prevent her from having an abortion if she wants one. They are not the least bit interested in protecting the newly born child or the mother who brought it into the world. Also many right-to-lifers also just so happen to believe in capital punishment. How is that consistent? It's okay to kill a grown man or woman, but absolutely not okay to destroy an unborn fetus a woman cannot afford to support. No legislation will ever prevent women from having abortions. They will return to back alleys and other dangerous situations. All the Texas legislators are doing is putting on full display their contempt for women. We will not forget when we next go to the voting booth."

This is from Robin:

"I was not able to have kids myself, so there was never a question of my needing an abortion. My son is adopted. His birth mother was only 15 when she got pregnant. I am glad my son's birth mother didn't have an abortion either. That is what was right for her and ultimately because of her love and generosity her decision ended being more than right for me too. But I stand firmly for each woman in Texas consulting her own conscience, the God of her own understanding, her own family, and her own doctor when she finds out she is expecting. No woman should have to consult with the Texas legislature over something so intensely personal, so life-altering and so spiritual. Politics is not everything. Some decisions are too important for politics. The life of a child is one of those things. So I ask you to stay real steady in fighting for the right of every woman to choose the path that is best for her, according to her own values and ideals and dreams. Some women dream of having a child; some dream of having a child later. Some women dream of being free from children so they can lift their family out of poverty, so they can go to or finish school. Some women are just too young to have their own children and don't have a family or a church who will pay for the child and help. Texas needs to go forward toward the future, not backward. It's a [ ] who cares about all women and not just the ones who agree with me. Robin."

This is from Patricia:

"Nearly 21 years ago I determined that I was pregnant. I had lost the love of my life many months before and was a little bit crazy, which led to the pregnancy. My first thought was to schedule an abortion, which I did. Upon further contemplation I decided that I could support a child and I wanted to do so. I was 39 years old at the time. I was concerned about potential issues related to my age, so I had a lot of tests done and decided to have the child. It was my decision and my decision alone. All of my family and friends supported me, but the important fact is that it was my decision. This is how it should be. My child and I made it. Every woman should have the opportunity to make the choice that's right for her."

From Harold:

"I am old enough to remember when women were driven to seek unlawful and unsafe abortions, often suffering complications, and I clearly remember one death in my community. Women should have control over their bodies. The provisions to ensure safety for women are unnecessary and are there to limit access for those least able to negotiate the steps necessary to obtain what they need. Those who claim to want to decrease abortions have also hampered the ability to obtain information on birth control and family planning. They are hypocrites."

This from someone who did not sign their name:

"With this bill Republicans are setting this state back 60 years. I believe in a woman's right to make choices for her own body, ultimately a choice that would affect her, the child, and society as whole for a lifetime. It saddens me to know that some poor woman, young or old would be essentially priced-out by the restrictions set forth in this bill. In a state as large as Texas, how can a woman receive fair quality, equitable medical-care. I can only imagine the costs associated with having to go to a surgery center for an abortion. Several years ago my sister, a single parent of one, found herself facing an unplanned pregnancy. Although the decision was agonizing for her, she made the difficult choice to abort the fetus. While not in complete agreement, I did support her right to make that decision for her life, and her future. So I was the one who took her to the clinic, held her hand and supported her in the months that followed. I would have been devastated had that option not been available or affordable for her, or even worse if our only other option would have been some back-alley clinic. Oh the mere thought of it right now brings me to tears. I urge each and every member of the Texas senate to put aside their own personal agendas, and do what their constituents desire, and what is right for women, children, and society."

And this from Brenda:

"I am a Christian, and an adoptive mother. The only way I could become a mother was for another woman to give birth and unselfishly give me her baby. I was so blessed that someone made that sacrifice for me. However, with that said, I strongly feel that every woman should have the right to do what they feel is best for themselves. Having an abortion is deeply personal, and should nev—and no one should have to answer to anyone but God. Since Rick Perry and David Dewhurst did not make the ultimate sacrifice for our sins, they have no right to tell anyone what they can and cannot do with their bodies. Women who choose to have an abortion should not be made to feel any worse than they already do by protesters, and they are entitled to good medical care, not second-rate clinics. When men can bear children, then they can make decisions on laws that would affect women. Thank you so much for standing up for women's rights. I will support you in every possible way."

This from Joy in Fort Worth:

"I am shocked and appalled at the workings of the Texas legislature; to deny women the right to adequate health-care while claiming to raise the standard of care for women is deceitful. I am so filled with concern for the plight of all women in the state of Texas, especially those who will now no longer have health services available to them, even those health services that some may find wrong. My mother worked in an abortion clinic for years. She worked with the women, mothers, daughters, husbands, and families that were faced with the choice of having to terminate a pregnancy. She believed strongly in what she did and to this day says that the counseling work that she did there was the most rewarding and valuable work she ever did. The women who visited the clinic where she worked were often harassed on their way to the clinic to make what was undoubtedly a difficult and agonizing decision. What I learned from her experience there was that one should never judge the motives of another. One of the stories that my mom told me has always stuck with me. She had a young devoutly religious couple visit her clinic. They already had a number of children and knew that they could not support anymore and had no family around that could assist them. During the counseling session, one of the two young couples told my mother that God would understand. It doesn't get more powerful or clear than that. So many of the decisions that we make in our lives are truly between God, and us, and nobody else. This is something that I've carried with me as a guiding principle all of my life."

From Ellen:

"My birthday is January 22nd, and I'll be celebrating my 65th year. As I do every year I also celebrate the day Roe v. Wade was passed. This provided all women the ability to get a chance to make the personal choice about her body and her life. As a registered nurse I've seen the result of backstreet abortions. We don't ever want to go back to those terrible days. I would never assume that I know what another person believes or wants so neither does anyone know what is good for me or my family. I have a daughter and a granddaughter, and all I want for them is for them to have a choice, with their position to make the decision that is right for them."

And this from Jessica in Arlington:

"As a person of deep faith, and I am enraged, with the continuing war on women especially when it comes to the banning of my healthcare dealing with abortions in Senate Bill 5. As a Christian I believe all life is sacred. The earth population is over 7 billion people and our planet is hurting. I grew up in the church. Members of my family are and have been leaders in the faith community. I was taught that the Bible talks about the oppression of women yet the good news was told to them first. Protecting life does not start or end in the womb. Supporting family planning is fully pro-life. Unfortunately too many members of the senate do not recognize women's rights or women's reproductive health issues. Family planning is comprehensive sex education, female empowerment, education, adoption, contraception, and fostering parenting initiatives. In addition, it is also testing and treatment for STD's and cancer, which protects women's' ability to have and care for children, and clinics do not have to be at a hospital level to be safe. Too much government control, limiting access to abortions, only drives them underground and puts women and who they care for and their health at risk. If governor Perry and others on the state legislature truly care about the health of its citizens, especially our sisters, mothers, grandmothers, daughters, and wives, they would have focused on expanding Medicaid, not restricting women's reproductive health. Particularly when over half the births in Texas are paid by medical aid, is this being good stewards of our state funds? Family planning is the way to reduce unwanted pregnancies and abortions and it protects religious freedom. Harsh restrictions on abortion are stepping on women's constitutional rights to control their bodies. Like Senate Bill 5. Many of us who are pro-choice want to work to reduce the number of abortions. We just can't have a fundamental part of our health be banned. Members of the state senate please stop the overreaching role of government in my life, my faith, and vote no on all of this bill."

This is from Valeda:

"I find it ironic that on a day when we were learning from the Annie E. Casey foundation that Texas once again ranks in the bottom 10 for child well-being, that the legislate was inserting themselves into the relationship between a woman and her doctor. Are there not enough challenges for the legislature? Is our education system fixed? Is our air clean? Are our roads totally smooth? I am old enough to remember what happened to women who did not get proper medical care. Every one of us today knows someone who's made the lonely drive to seek medical advice. The decision is not an easy one as that person talks with her doctor, her loved one, her family, a friend, her faith leader, and yes, God. Why must the legislature insert politics and ignorance into these discussions? Why must rural and poor women disproportionately bear the greatest burden of the heavy weight of politics? I hope the legislature stands up to the pressure of a few and responds to the call of many. Reject the inaccuracies and the hate, and do not pass this legislation."

This is from Andrea:

"We lost our 24-year-old niece who became pregnant, but after about 5 months her body was rejecting the fetus. She was throwing up blood clots for several days but the hospital would not abort the fetus, claiming they did not know what was causing the difficulty. We ended up losing them both. We will never know if she could have been saved, but the option of expeditiously making that sort of painful decision should always be available to us, without our government legislators standing in the way, this being the most intimate of places between a woman and her doctor, and they have no right to force themselves into that private space, ever."

From James:

"There should be no laws preventing access to medical care. Protect our god given right to choose our destiny for ourselves."

From Candy:

"There are so many stories from the days before abortions were legal and safe, as they should remain, because no matter how many laws are put on the books, women will always have abortions and have had for thousands of years. I have never been in the position to need or have an abortion, but I have way too many friends who have gone down that road, often because they were forced to have abortions by their husbands, or their parents. This was before birth control was readily available and abortions were legal. I have a friend who's 60 now; she got pregnant at 15, her father brought a fireman home to perform her abortion in her bedroom. She never had children. I have another friend who was also pregnant as a teenager, whose father put her on a bus at the age of 15 with an address in New York City and told her not to come home until it was done. These are just a few of the many stories . . . the friend who got pregnant in the early seventies, and because her parents had money, was able to get on an airplane, so she went to New York City where abortion was accessible. I don't know if she chose that abortion or if her parents did. The friend that got pregnant after her first sexual experience at 18, all went to New York, that liberal bastion, thank God it was there, or who knows what would have happened to these women. College girls taken across the border to Mexico for their abortions. The list goes on and on and on. All this law will do is harm and prevent women from a safe abortion. It won't stop them from having one. The point is that an abortion should be a choice, made in private, with a woman's doctor . . . Not a choice made by a parent, a husband or a government, because a government that tells you that you must have a child, can also be a government that tells you cannot have a child, and when that occurs we become a place like China."

From Paula:

"I don't have a story of personal loss or agony regarding choice. You see, I am a wife, middle class woman and I have the freedom of choice that money provides. The proposed legislation is an assault on poor women, probably most often poor women of color. I feel a powerlessness in all of this, and this is when I don't feel the bile of disgust and anger welling up. But, you know, I can't even begin to imagine how this feels to a young African American or Latino woman who is hearing this from old white legislators. I ask you to speak my words, share my thoughts, and in some small way help me make a difference with this body of legislators, who despite their partisan leanings, have taken an oath to represent us, all of us, and vote our will, not theirs."

From Robin:

"I had an abortion when I was 23. It was a horrible experience for me but it was a necessary decision. I was able to do that because there were affordable clinics. I grew up going to Planned Parenthood and got my annual screenings and birth control. Please stay strong and speak for all of us women in Texas. I have been a nurse for over 40 years and I now work in

Home Health. I see on a daily basis what happens when poor under- or uninsured people don't have access to the healthcare that we all deserve."

This one's not signed:

"The words 'freedom to choose' summarize our position. My wife and I have two wonderful daughters and an adopted grandchild. If there were an unwanted pregnancy in our family we would have serious reservations about choosing an abortion. However, it is a very personal choice, and we would never impose our views on our daughters or on strangers. Allowing abortions up to a reasonable time, for example 24 weeks, and at a larger—at a large number of affordable, safe locations makes sense to us. We could afford to fly to another state if abortions were banned in Texas. However, many other families are less fortunate and would not have this option. Let us hope that the latest anti-abortion bill is not passed, and that more reasonable viewpoints prevail in Austin."

This one is from someone named Robin:

"I was in Austin yesterday, came from DC, but had to head back. I had an abortion in Houston a few years ago when my birth control failed due to antibiotics given after a surgery for cervical cancer. Because of health problems I've had: ovarian cysts, endometriosis, cervical cancer, and the surgeries I've had to treat them, carrying a pregnancy could be extremely dangerous both for me and for the fetus. Procedures to address my cervical cancer have compromised the strength of my cervix—. Later in a pregnancy it's possible my cervix wouldn't be able to hold a full uterus. But we couldn't know; if I had carried the pregnancy and developed complications, I would likely have had to abort in order to save my life and any possible future fertility. It would have been well past 20 weeks. My doctors have told me that any pregnancy for me will be very high risk. I was only 23, in a relationship with someone who didn't treat me very well, and far from any family, emotional, or financial support. Carrying that pregnancy just wasn't possible. And women that face those same complications don't only live in Houston, Austin, San Antonio, and Dallas. They live all over the state, in rural areas with limited contraception access and high rates of teen pregnancy. They live in Oklahoma and Louisiana where the closest clinic, by far, is in Texas. All women need access to abortion, whether healthy or not, whether a rape victim or not, whether they have the financial resources to raise a child or not. Republicans would now tell me that I couldn't follow my doctor's advice. They should be ashamed of themselves for preaching about freedom from government intrusion, while stepping quite literally between me and my doctor."

And now members I want to talk about the misplaced priorities that this bill represents. SP-5 is merely the latest attack in what can only be characterized as a war on women's health in this state. Steps taken by the legislature during the 82nd regular session helped pave the way for these most recent attempts to limit family planning and reproductive health services. An article in the Austin chronicle from April 22nd, 2011, lays out the dramatic actions taken by the legislature to defund Planned Parenthood, which results, of course, in an increase of unplanned births and more women who will confront the difficulties that are presented by virtue of SP-5. I want to read from that article. It was titled "The War on Women's Health: To Attack Planned Parenthood, Lawmakers Undermine Healthcare and Promote More Abortions." It was written on April 22nd, 2011, by Jordan Smith:

"On April 1st following several hours of intense floor debate in the Texas House on a string of budget amendments seeking to reallocate funds designated to provide basic women's healthcare services, the dust was settling. Conservative Republicans claimed victory: Seven amendments had successfully stripped from the roughly $99 million dollar pot almost $62 million intended to fulfill the state's commitment to provide family-planning and reproductive health services for thousands of low-income, uninsured women. Meanwhile, another successful amendment enacted a funding matrix designating to which healthcare providers, and in what order, the remaining funds would be allocated—a move designed specifically to yank public funds from Planned Parenthood. Foes of reproductive choice with the statewide group Texas Right to Life were quick to post to the group's website a self-congratulatory statement taking credit for dismantling the state's family-planning program. Quote: 'Texas Right to Life removes 61 million tax funds from abortion industry!' proclaimed the headline. Indeed, says TRL's Elizabeth Graham, her organization helped lawmakers orchestrate a strategy to strip the family-planning program of as much of its federal funding as is legally allowable. 'Spearheading that effort means that members of the legislature had come to Texas Right to Life asking about family-planning revenues and how to take money away from abortions,' she said during a recent interview, and 'to redirect the funds to more deserving and more worthy programs.' With a 27 billion dollar state budget deficit for existing services, there's no shortage of underfunded programs and some of the programs to which the family planning funds were diverted are certainly worthy. One amendment moved funds to mental healthcare for children, for example, while another diverted funds to services for children with multiple disabilities. Yet conservative opponents of family planning, including TRL and the amendment sponsors, refused to acknowledge that none of the federal money the state has traditionally used to fund women's reproductive healthcare is used to fund abortion services. Federal law expressly prohibits using the funds for that purpose. Instead, the funds used for family planning provide low-income women with guaranteed access to very basic health services—including annual gynecological exams, counseling on pregnancy planning and access to birth control, screening for breast and cervical cancers, testing for hypertension and tuberculosis, and screening for sexually transmitted infections, including HIV. Taken together, these preventive services make up what is commonly referred to as a 'well woman check.' For hundreds of thousands of Texas women the services provided with these funds represent their only regular and reliable access to medical care. Not surprisingly, therefore, advocates for women's healthcare viewed the debate somberly. 'Devastating,' said Fran Hagerty, CEO of the Women's Health and Family Planning Association of Texas, a group that represents a diverse mix of 58 family-planning providers across Texas. 'There will be very quick consequences for the state,' she says—including increased cost for unplanned pregnancies, costlier cancer treatments begun in later stages of disease, and ironically, a likely increase in the number of abortions. The facts about what the federal money actually pays for—and the long-term risks and costs of failing to fund these preventive health services—have not prevented anti-abortion lawmakers and advocates from alleging that the opposite is true. Some simply ignore the facts (TRL insists that family planning funds are merely 'blood money'), while others draw a direct line from family-planning funding to abortion via their favorite target, Planned Parenthood. In fact the vast majority of the 90-year-old non-profit's services are dedicated to preventive healthcare, and less than 5% of its Texas operations, not supported by government funds, involve legally protected abortion services. That remains too much for these staunch defenders of life. For years Texas lawmakers have declared that they would love nothing more than to defund Planned Parenthood entirely, regardless of the effect that it would have on the larger women's healthcare network, and this year, with the GOP supermajority at the capital, the rhetoric has been ratcheted up. The assault on family-planning funding in Texas is just one symptom of this singular focus nationwide. In Washington D.C. GOP lawmakers recently tried and failed to ram through a budget amendment authored by Indiana representative Mike Pence to ban Planned Parenthood from getting any federal funding for any purpose whatsoever; they're not about to quit the fight. Concurrently, conservative lawmakers propose cutting all funding for teen pregnancy prevention programs and for Title Ten, the 41-year-old source of revenue dedicated to women's health services, and the one pot of money that Texas lawmakers are powerless to divert to other programs. 'They're going after women's health,' said Cecile Richards, president of the Planned Parenthood

Federation of America, during a February press call. 'This is the most extreme assault on women in decades. They want to eliminate vital healthcare for more than 5 million America women,' served by Planned Parenthood, including 3 million women its clinic serve nationwide using Title Ten funds. The Texas senate has yet to debate its somewhat less draconian budget draft, but whatever the differences between the chambers that remain to be hashed out before final passage, it is clear that thousands of low-income and uninsured women will have little or no access to healthcare for at least the next two years. Amid all the supposedly high-minded and abstract debate about where life begins, one overwhelming reality is all too easily ignored. What is misleadingly described as 'defunding the abortion industry' is in fact the wholesale shredding of the healthcare safety net for women, in Texas and in the U.S. In Texas, attacks on funding for women's healthcare are nothing new, and the specific attacks on Planned Parenthood are as old as the organization itself. 'No question, Planned Parenthood has been around for 90 years. From day one we've had a handful of folks who didn't think birth control should be legal,' says Sarah Wheat, vice president of communications for Planned Parenthood of the Texas Capital Region. Those attacks have come from foes of birth control, of equal treatment for women, from those opposed to nonprocreative sex of any kind, and simply from opponents of abortion. 'We believe that women's health is important, and that women and families are healthier when pregnancies are planned and spaced,' Wheat says, 'Healthcare should be just as accessible and affordable for low-income women as it is for the rest.' Planned Parenthood takes that commitment seriously, and over time it has come to be the nation's leading provider of reproductive healthcare for women. At one time or another, 20% of women nationwide have used Planned Parenthood's services. Currently, the organization operates more than 800 clinics across the country, performs a million pap tests, and more than 800 thousand breast exams each year, both critical to the early detection of cancer, and provides nearly 4 million tests and treatments for sexually transmitted infections. These preventive services, combined with dispensing birth control to more than 2.5 million women annually, help each year to prevent more than 600 thousand unplanned pregnancies, according to Planned Parenthood's statistics. According to the federal government, one dollar invested in family-planning services saves taxpayers nearly four dollars in other healthcare costs. In 2010 alone, more that 260,000 Texas women, men, and teens were served by the state's 81 Planned Parenthood clinics. More than 120,000 were screened for cervical and breast cancers, and more than 380,000 received testing and treatment for STI's. In 2010 more than a quarter of Planned Parenthood's Texas patients were low-income women, served by the state's pass-through of federal funding, including from the state's pot of Title Ten funds. Planned Parenthood is not the only provider of healthcare for low-income Texas women. Each year some 78 contractors across Texas, funding roughly 286 providers, received federal funds allocated by the state to provide this basic care. In fiscal year 2010, these providers used roughly 47.6 million dollars in funds to provide basic healthcare to a total of 257,895 low-income clients. Of these groups, the public providers saw the most clients at just more than 86,000, 37% of all low-income reproductive health clients served with these funds, but at $219, these group's costs per client was higher than that of Planned Parenthood. The other contractors include city and county health departments, hospitals, community health centers, like Austin People's Community Clinic, stand-alone family planning clinics, and federally qualified health centers. However, Planned Parenthood's long institutional history has allowed the organization to hone its delivery of preventive reproductive healthcare to women across the country and in Texas, making it uniquely able to provide services in a cost effective manner in even the most isolated communities. Last year, Planned Parenthood clinics in Texas used federal funds to see more than 73,000 patients, at an average cost of just $168 per client. These economic realities haven't prevented lawmakers from trying to find a way to defund Planned Parenthood. Before the session the last major attack came in the 2005 legislative session in a budget rider authored by Sen. Robert Deuell, R-Greenville. Deuell walks an interesting line on women's healthcare. He's a doctor. And neither the benefits of preventative care nor the needs of women are lost on him. Deuell is openly hostile toward Planned Parenthood, though his explicit reasoning is supposedly magnanimous. Planned Parenthood's services are limited and occupy a niche, he argues. And the state should focus its limited healthcare dollars on first funding more comprehensive medical providers, namely federally qualified health senators—centers. These FQHCs aim to serve any and all indigent clients in need of a medical home, serving as a portal for care for a variety of health services, such as mental health and dental care, in addition to reproductive health. Lawmakers approved the Deuell rider, directing the Department of State Health Services to direct 10 million each year from the state's family planning money first to fund FQHCs before allocating the remaining money to the rest of the state's providers, including Planned Parenthood clinics. This would seem to make sense, providing low-income patients a single point of entry for medical care is not a bad thing. In practice, however, it hasn't helped to expand access to care. For starters, there are fewer than 70 FQHCs across the state, and because they aim to address so many different health issues for a needy population, many of them are already bursting with patients. The rider took effect beginning with the 2006 funding cycle, and the consequences were immediate. That year alone, more than 41,000 fewer women were provided with reproductive healthcare funded by three main pots of federal money: Title V, the maternal and child health block grant, Title XX, the social services block grant, and Title X. Together, the three provide services for women not eligible for Medicaid. In the following year, more than 28,000 women lost services according to Hagerty of the Women's Health and Planning Association of Texas, who regularly compiles statistics and crunches numbers provided by DSHS and the health and human service commission that pertains to women's healthcare. The FQHCs simply could not absorb the clients who were hemorrhaged from the more traditional family planning providers that lost funding because of the FQHC allocation. And the FQHCs that have received funding have not been able to spend all of it, each year returning a significant amount of money to the state for reallocation. And though the 2006 FQHCs that are now receiving funding for these services have steadily increased the amount of money they are using, their average cost per client is $225, so they're still not picking up nearly as many clients as have lost care since the imposition of the Deuell funding scheme. In 2010, FQHCs processed 13% of clients for reproductive health funded by family planning dollars, according to DSHS."

And of course, this is part of why so many are concerned about Senate Bill 5. The fewer dollars being directed particularly toward reproductive healthcare, the need for those services, abortion services, has risen, and with that need, of course, the consequences of Senate Bill 5 becoming even greater. I return to reading the article.

"In short, say healthcare advocates, if the intention was indeed to improve access to healthcare, the Deuell plan hasn't worked out so well. 'Put simply,' says Randall Ellis, Senior Director of Government Relations for the well respected Houston FQHC Legacy Community Health Services, 'it takes the entire spectrum of providers, including Planned Parenthood, to meet the needs of the growing population of low-income people without access to reproductive and other basic healthcare services. We work in conjunction with Planned Parenthood for family planning, and HIV services. We do referrals back and forth so that people can receive services in the setting that they're most comfortable in,' he said. 'These family planning providers, providers that specialize in family planning services, provide these services in a much more cost effective manner than do the other providers without the know-how, much more cost effectively than Legacy or the other FQHCs that don't have the background or expertise in providing healthcare.' These facts on the ground have done nothing to prompt lawmakers to reconsider the allocation scheme and things are about to get worse."

And of course members, we know they did.

"While Deuell's approach might be well-intended and based on his medical experience, the same cannot be said of most of the folks who have jumped on the funding scheme train. Those include prominent foes of abortion, most without medical background or healthcare expertise, whose primary objective reflects no desire to see that as many low-income women as possible have access to basic healthcare, but only that Planned Parenthood be defunded, as the visible incarnation of the abortion industry. During testimony at a House Human Services Committee Hearing last month, Joe Pojman, executive director of Austin-based Texas Alliance for Life, argued passionately that defunding Planned Parenthood would open up the doors to other providers: FQHCs and actual private physicians to accept Medicaid to serve women. 'These are where our tax dollars should be spent,' he told the committee. 'Don't women in Texas deserve better care? If Planned Parenthood in Texas was defunded, those women will be far better off because they would be given a medical home.'"

And members, to depart from this for a moment, and share a personal experience that I had, with Planned Parenthood, starting when I was in my late teens, Planned Parenthood became my medical home. It was my only medical home, and had it not been for the Planned Parenthood clinic on Henderson Street in Fort Worth, Texas, I wouldn't have been able to access any sort of care for myself, not contraception, not blood pressure tests, not cancer screening tests. None of that would've been available to me, because I was a poor, uninsured woman, whose only care was provided through that facility. It was my medical home. To return to the article:

"The rallying cry of Pojman and others, dismissing the reality of how the funding is actually being allocated, has been bolstered this year by the addition of a charismatic new voice. Abby Johnson, former director of a Planned Parenthood clinic in Bryan, Texas, left that job and joined the pro-life movement she says, after she witnessed during an ultrasound-guided abortion procedure, a fetus struggle not to be terminated. Johnson is young, charming, and well-spoken, although there are serious questions about the veracity of her tale. She blames Planned Parenthood for trying to discredit her. 'The holes in the story don't come from me,' she insists. Johnson has been embraced by pro-lifers who see Planned Parenthood as an especially nefarious evildoer, simply a portal through which the stated goal of providing healthcare is in fact secondary to somehow enticing women facing unplanned pregnancies into abortion. Johnson promotes that notion. At least half of the women in her clinic seeking abortion care had been using contraception when they got pregnant. 'Therefore,' she claims, 'Planned Parenthood may be good at providing birth control to the masses, but not at providing good contraceptive and related education. That's a pretty significant problem. Their health education is promoting sex without consequences, which ultimately is what abortion is really about,' she says. Johnson also argues that if Planned Parenthood is taken out of the funding mix, plenty of providers will pick up the slack. Asked about the experiences over the last few years under the Deuell rider, Johnson responds that it simply doesn't go far enough. The problem, she argues, is that under his rider, Planned Parenthood remains eligible for some funding, and that still is siphoning funds away from other providers. Additional FQHCs, and public health entities, for example, that might otherwise be able to provide more comprehensive services including reproductive healthcare. 'So I'm not concerned where these women would go,' she says. 'It's not just FQHCs, it's rural health services, community hospitals, there are 10 to 20 times the number of places that women could go for care.' Johnson says that while you can't deny that Planned Parenthood does provide healthcare to low-income women, those services are too limited in scope to be an appropriate recipient of tax dollars. 'What I try to reiterate is that while they are providing those good services, they are also providing more than 320,000 abortions each year in the US,' she says. Johnson insists that she is not a hardcore conservative. She isn't just pro-life. 'I say I'm pro quality of life—I'm for social programs,' she says. 'It doesn't just stop at birth for me. Women, men and children should get healthcare that they deserve and that they need.' So while she supports defunding Planned Parenthood, she's against any move to take money away from providing reproductive healthcare to low-income people such as the proposal in Congress to eliminate Title 10. 'I am not for any kind of restrictions on funding that would take away money from women who need services. I don't want money, tax money, to go to clinics that perform abortion services,' she says, 'but I'm not in any way in favor of taking money away from health services.' Unfortunately, despite Johnson's demurrals, defunding healthcare is in actual fact of the current plan in Texas. Under the seven budget amendments passed this month in the Texas House, there will be very little left to fund reproductive health services at all. In the effort to attack Planned Parenthood, lawmakers have thrown the proverbial baby out with the bathwater. The amendments stripped nearly 62 million over the biennial from family planning, moving virtually all Title 5 and Title 10 money to other strategies, each move presumably allowable under federal law. What is left is only the biennial funds allocated for Title 10 money, that lawmakers could not redirect from reproductive heath services. In all, there's roughly 38 million left for 2 years. With the Deuell rider still in effect, that means there's 18 million over the biennium, just 9 million per year, to provide money to the more than 50 non-FQHC contractors currently serving more than 227,000 women. Since 2005, those providers have had access to between roughly 35 million and 40 million a year to provide service to these women, who are but a fraction of the hundreds of thousands of women who actually need services in Texas. With Texas's dubious claim to fame as the state with the highest percentage of uninsured people, about 26% in 2009 according to the Kaiser Family Foundation, the number of women in need of reproductive healthcare is roughly 1.5 million, according to the Guttmacher Institute. Moreover, in an attempt to deliver a deathblow to Planned Parenthood, conservative lawmakers also approved an eighth amendment, offered by Representative Warren Chisum, that expands the 2005 Deuell funding rider by spelling out how the remaining 9 million per year should be allocated. First, the money would go to public entities that provide family planning, including community clinics and county and city health departments. Second in line would be non-public entities that provide comprehensive primary and preventative care in addition to reproductive health services. Third, whatever is left, under the presumption of course that there won't be anything left, would go to non-public entities that provide only reproductive healthcare, including Planned Parenthood. Texas Right to Life's Graham was nearly giddy about the amendment and the postings of the TRL website. 'The final amendment earned 113 votes to snatch the last 9 million,' she wrote. In an interview with the Texas Tribune prior to the debate, Representative Sid Miller, author of the Ultrasound Before Abortion bill that the house passed in March, foreshadowed the floor debate. 'I would say Planned Parenthood would have a tough time getting any government funds, state funds—'"

Dewhurst: Senator Nichols for what purpose do you ask.

Senator Nichols: Mr. President, under rule 4.03, is the budget germane to this bill?

Dewhurst: No.

Nichols: I think she's talking about the budget.

Davis: Mr. President, may I please argue my point with regards to its germaneness, and if you rule that it's not, I'm happy to move onto something else. But in the debate over Senate Bill 5, umm, I did argue of course, about restoring the women's health program funding. I made the argument and actually introduced an amendment to Senate Bill 5 that would have restored the women's health program in Texas. Right now, as you know, we have completely turned away those dollars and we've done so because in order to take them, we would have to provide them to providers like Planned Parenthood. I made the argument that we were giving up about $30 million in federal funds that could've otherwise been brought down for preventing abortion, which of course, is the topic of this bill. And of course, and because I introduced the amendment, it was voted on and declined, I believed that this was relevant to the discussion on this bill.

[*Pause.*]

Dewhurst: Senator . . . mmm. I don't think . . . I don't think that the contents and the subject matter of the funding of Planned Parenthood is . . . is germane to this debate, and please consider this as a warning and if you could keep your comments to Senate Bill 5 and the elements in, in the bill and the subject of abortion. Thank you senator.

Davis: Thank you Mr. President. [*Pause.*] At this time, I'd like to talk about alternatives to abortion through prevention, and again, a very lengthy part of our conversation on Senate Bill 5 had to do with its failure in the name of women's health to address women's healthcare in a way that would prevent the need for abortions. The *Houston Chronicle* had a good article on that, dated March 14th, 2013.

"When it comes to a woman's right to choose, reasonable minds would agree that a decline in abortion rates should bode well for all of us. Every child should be a wanted child. However, the most recent study on the issue, showing that in the past two years, Texas abortion rates have declined by 10–15%, presents a more complicated picture. The national rate has been declining also, but not as sharply. Preliminary results as reported by the *Chronicle* study, 'Abortions on Decline in Texas,' shows that the drop is steeper in Texas, not because fewer women are choosing abortion, but because the draconian budget cuts and punitive measures from the 2011 session are creating obstacles."

Dewhurst: Senator Nichols, for what purpose do you rise.

Nichols: A question, a point of order on rule 4.03, under the germaneness . . . I don't think alternatives to abortions are related to Senate Bill 5.

[*Pause.*]

Dewhurst: Senator Nichols, as long as Senator Davis is on the subject of abortion, I think that is related to the subject matter of Senate Bill 5, but let me . . . umm, I'll be glad to revisit that with you . . . I'll, I'll . . . we'll continue to listen to the debate.

Nichols: Thank you.

Davis: I'll continue where I left off in the article. "In a rush—

Dewhurst: [*Unintelligible*]

Davis: " . . . to stamp out abortion, our state leaders are also wreaking havoc on the most practical common sense mechanisms for avoiding unplanned pregnancies in the first place. Namely, widespread affordable access to family planning services. In an appallingly short-sighted measure, lawmaker's last session slashed state family planning funding by two-thirds from 115 million to 37.9 million resulting in the closing of more than half of the state funded clinics. By the end of last year, state researchers were predicting that due to this lost funding, births in the 14 by 15 biennium would increase by about 24,000 and will cost taxpayers up to an additional 233 . . . 273 million. Researchers in the latest study of several hundred women seeking abortions found that in about 90% of cases, the women did not change their minds after compiling with the new demands—more evidence that our energies and our tax dollars should be focused on family planning services, not on creating more hurdles for women at a time when they are already facing a daunting choice. That there is hope that reason is beginning to prevail . . .

Dewhurst: Senator Watson, for what purpose do you rise?

Senator Watson: Without Senator Davis yielding the floor, I wonder if she would yield for some questions.

Davis: I will yield for questions without yielding the floor, thank you Senator.

Watson: Thank you Mr. President . . . Senator Davis, umm, I apologize for interrupting, but I was hopeful that we could talk a moment and I could ask you some questions about some of the legal aspects to the abortion, uh, issue and start, if we could, with a case that has been mentioned by you and others on the floor, of *Roe v. Wade*.

Davis: Yes.

Watson: You're familiar with the year that was decided.

Davis: Yes, I have the case in front of me. It was decided in—it was argued 1971, and decided January 22nd, 1973.

Watson: And in that case, you're probably familiar, as part of your legal background, with the fact that there had been issues in, uh, previous cases of, issues like this of being able to get in the courts because there were questions raised about standing, because pregnancies last only a certain period of time. The woman would be pregnant . . . she would end up having the baby, then she would end uh, uh, up not having standing.

Davis: That's correct.

Watson: Correct? And so one of the issues that came up in the case of *Roe v. Wade* was, um, that the usual rule in federal cases was that an actual controversy had to exist at the stages of the appellate, uh, or the review *on cert*, and not simply at the date the action was initiated. So if the woman were pregnant, there would be a period of time where the case would be ongoing, she would have her baby, then on appeal or on the review *on cert*, she would no longer be pregnant. And as I understand it, it is your understanding that would then moot the case.

Davis: Right.

Watson: And so some of these cases weren't able to make it to where there was review about what was the constitutional right of women.

Davis: That's right, it was quite a, quite a challenge.

Watson: As the court pointed out in the case of *Roe v. Wade*, and, and, I, I would cite you to headnote 4 in that case that they pointed out that with human gestation they've come to term before the appeal could be completed, and so in this case, is it your understanding what the United States Supreme Court said is that they could rule in the case because they finally determined that pregnancy provides a classic justification for a conclusion of non-mootness because it truly could be capable of repetition yet evading review?

Davis: That's exactly what they decided.

Watson: Senator, one of the big issues that had not been decided prior to the case of *Roe v. Wade*, is that in the instances of, of, of, a termination of a pregnancy, is whether or not that in fact was protected and, by the United States Constitution, and once the court was able to get past the issue of whether or not it was moot, is it your understanding that the court actually addressed the issue so that we had some definition on whether a woman's right to make that decision was constitutionally protected?

Davis: That's right, for the first time.

Watson: And, is it your understanding in the case of *Roe v. Wade*, the principle thrust of the appellant's argument in that case, or in fact, their attack on the Texas statute that made certain terminations of pregnancy a crime, is that it improperly invaded a right said to be possessed by a pregnant woman to choose to terminate her pregnancy?

Davis: That's correct.

Watson: In fact, that's the exact language of *Roe v. Wade*, is that the thrust of the argument was that it improperly invaded a right said to be possessed by the pregnant woman to choose to terminate her pregnancy.

Davis: That's correct.

Watson: Um, and is it your understanding that in the case, when the court reviewed this case, that it pointed out that the appellant, or in this case, the woman who was being charged with a crime, uh, that they would discover this right in the concept of personal liberty?

Davis: That's correct, that was the constitutional underpinning of their position.

Watson: So, so, what you're saying is that the constitutional underpinning in *Roe v. Wade* was that the woman's right possessed—that she possessed—it, it, invaded a right that she possessed was based on the concept of personal liberty, and is it your understanding that what the court found embodied that personal liberty was embodied in the 14th Amendment's due process clause.

Davis: That's correct.

Watson: Or the argument was that it was found in personal merit familial and sexual privacy that said to be protected by the bill of rights or its penumbras.

Davis: That's correct.

Dewhurst: Senator Nichols, for what reason do you rise sir?

Nichols: I ask a question under 4.03, germaneness, it is my understanding that all questions have to be with, with regards to the body of the bill. I don't quite understand what part of the bill his question relates to.

Watson: May I reply?

Dewhurst: You may.

Watson: The whole issue here is whether or not—uh, when we're talking about abortion, we're talking about the underpinnings of personal liberty. We're talking about a woman's right to make choices. We're talking about the seminal case that gives rise to that recognition of personal liberty in *Roe v. Wade*.

Nichols: Mr. President, that is not the body of the bill—

Dewhurst: [*Unintelligible*] The Senate rule 4.03 deals with . . . with, with the issue before us. The issue before is Senate Bill 5, so I'm going to sustain the motion and ask that you stay on the subject of this bill and how it works . . . and . . . and as tightly construed as you can, a discussion on abortion.

Nichols: Mr. President . . . is that a warning?

Dewhurst: That's a second warning.

Nichols: Thank you.

Davis: Well, Mr President, I'm not sure that that's a second warning under the rule—

Dewhurst: I'm not calling you on a—

Davis: . . . because it's not a warning to me, the speaker.

Dewhurst: . . . I'm not calling you on a warning. I'm not calling you on a warning.

Davis: Thank you.

Watson: Let's be clear. If you're not calling Senator Davis on a warning, then that warning is to me.

Dewhurst: As simply that . . . that is correct. That . . . Please limit your questions to the subject of the legislation or the legislation. And as tightly construed to abortion as you can.

Senator West: Parliamentary inquiry.

Dewhurst: State your inquiry.

West: I'm just trying to make certain we understand the rules. Because we're hearing a bunch of warnings now. Under the rules, what impact would warnings of members have on Senator Davis's ability to continue her conversation about these bills.

Dewhurst: Senator West, the warning was to, to Senator Watson to confine his comments to the subject of the bill that is being debated. It has nothing to do with Senator Davis.

West: Okay, um, parliamentary inquiry.

Dewhurst: State your inquiry.

West: If Senator Davis is given three warnings, what impact does that have on her ability to maintain the floor?

[*Pause.*]

Dewhurst: Uh, Senator West, on the third point of order, that would be sustained, then it's not a warning, and it would be put to the body for a vote on whether to end the . . .

West: Parliamentary inquiry.

Dewhurst: State your inquiry.

West: What would that vote be? Is it two-thirds or simple majority?

Dewhurst: It's a simple majority.

West: Ok, so the third decision . . . the third warning upheld by the Lieutenant Governor would then put the issue to the body to decide whether or not to frankly pass the bill.

Dewhurst: Senator West, after the second warning to an individual, to a senator that' s conducting a filibuster, the next warning would be put to the . . . the next point of order, if sustained would be . . . is put to the body.

West: And that's from Senate Rule 4.03 and the precedent there under, or what?

Dewhurst: Yes.

West: OK. And that's to Senator Davis, that's not to an individual member?

Dewhurst: That is correct.

West: OK. Thank you, Mr. President.

Dewhurst: Senator Ellis, for what purpose do you rise, Sir?

Senator Ellis: Parliamentary inquiry, Mr. President.

Dewhurst: State your inquiry.

Ellis: Just to make sure I understand the nature of what questions I can ask in this filibuster: am I able to ask Senator Davis to read me sections of the committee substitute to Senate Bill 5, just to make sure that I don't stray from the subject at hand?

Dewhurst: The subject that would be germane to the debate is the subject of Senate Bill 5.

Ellis: So my parliamentary inquiry is, am I able to ask Senator Davis to read sections of the bill to me, slowly [*Laughter.*] . . . I just wanna make sure I can understand it. [*Pause.*]

Dewhurst: Senator Ellis, with all due respect, I'm not gonna issue a ruling that permits a debate that's not substantive. The subject is Senate Bill 5, um, and you know as well as I do that a proper question would be on Senate Bill 5.

Ellis: OK. I have a series of question about the committee substitute to Senate Bill 5, if it does not take Senator Davis off the floor.

Dewhurst: When the, when the parliamentary inquiry was first made, it was made by Senator Watson, and he was asking questions. Um, if Senator Watson wishes to continue asking . . .

Watson: I would.

Dewhurst: . . . questions then he has the floor. But first, I noticed . . . Senator Williams, for what purpose do you rise, Sir?

Senator Williams: [*Inaudible.*]

Dewhurst: OK. Senator Watson, you are recognized.

Watson: Thank you. Senator Davis, we were talking about *Roe v. Wade*, and I hear the presiding officer and President of the Senate's ruling on the point of order that was raised. Let me, let me bring it back to Senate Bill 5. In Senate Bill 5, is there a limitation . . . a time limitation . . . placed on when a woman would be allowed to have . . . to terminate a pregnancy?

Davis: Yes, Senate Bill 5 would prohibit an abortion past 20 weeks of gestation, and that gestational age itself, there is some argument about the way it's defined in the bill, um, saying that typically under medical practice it's practice to determine that date from the date of the last menstrual period, whereas here it's the date of the fertilization of the fetus. And as you heard earlier in some of the reports or the letters that I read from ACOG, they are very concerned about changing to a standard that probably moves the date even earlier than 20 weeks of gestation in terms of what would be prohibited in the abortion arena.

Watson: Well and yet, even in the case that we were talking about of *Roe v. Wade*, in that case the court, the Supreme Court, looked at when states could be involved in taking certain action that would perhaps . . . uh, could invade a woman's right to privacy and her constitutional right as it applies to the termination of her pregnancy, is that correct?

Davis: That's right, and they of course created a standard in that opinion, the standard being that states could not regulate or inhibit a woman's constitutional right to an abortion procedure um, prior to the viability of the fetus.

Watson: And again, to focus on SB 5, SB 5 . . . and I understand what you just said in the answer to the question that it might be less than 20 weeks, but SB 5 talks in terms of 20 weeks, and the United States Supreme Court in *Roe v. Wade* talked about a woman could terminate a pregnancy without interference by the state prior to approximately the end of the first trimester of the pregnancy.

Davis: That's correct.

Watson: They say 28 weeks, roughly 28 weeks is . . .

Davis: That's the second trimester.

Watson: I'm sorry, that's right. [*Crosstalk*.] So, there's a companion case to *Roe v. Wade*, is that correct?

Davis: That's right.

Watson: And that's a case that came out of Georgia called *Doe v. Bolton*.

Davis: That's correct.

Watson: And . . .

Dewhurst: Senator Nichols, for what purpose do you rise, Sir?

Nichols: Inquiry and point of order on point 4.03 again, germaneness. We're back to question related to *Roe v. Wade*, which is not a part of this bill, and it's my . . . also I have a question about, if the Senator whose . . . Davis is responding to a non-germane question, is that also included in the warning?

Watson: Mr. President, I have tied it specifically . . . my questions related to this case and the, the underpinnings of the law specifically to SB 5. [*Extended pause.*]

Dewhurst: Senator Watson, would you approach the podium? [*Extended pause.*]

Dewhurst: Senator Nichols, on the specific point of order that you raised, at the present time it's respectfully overruled. But, um, the debate needs to be kept to the subject of the bill, and we'll be . . . and I'm sure you'll be alert to that.

Nichols: Thank you. [*Pause.*]

Dewhurst: Senator Watson, you are recognized for questions.

Watson: Thank you, Mr. President. Uh, Senator Davis, when we were interrupted I was asking about the underpinnings of states, like the state of Texas, being able to put restrictions on the constitutionally recognized right of a woman to terminate the pregnancy. And, um, in SB 5, are there restrictions being placed, both literally and practically, on a woman's right to terminate . . . her, her constitutional right to terminate her pregnancy, as we've been talking about?

Davis: There are, and they come in several forms. As you know, this was an omnibus bill that included four new areas of law that would cover abortions in the state of Texas. One of those was in terms of the standard of what that facility needed to look like, and certainly an argument can be made that in the state of Texas, the consequence of the ambulatory surgical center provision of SB 5 will decrease, in a fairly dramatic form, the number of centers at which abortions can and will be provided in Texas. I would suspect that as has been the case in other states that have confronted that question, there will be lawsuits if this law were to go into . . . if this bill were to go into law. And *Roe v. Wade* is the . . . one of the . . . legal opinions to which any judge who is deciding the constitutionality of that provision would be allowable, because *Roe v. Wade* set a standard by which states must follow in terms of regulations that they put on abortion facilities, as did *Doe v. Bolton*, the other case that you referenced. There are three other pieces of this bill that would be subject to a review of the standards that were put in place in *Roe v. Wade*. One of those is the provision of the abortion drug, and how and when it can be administered. And in this bill, there are restrictions in terms of not only when it can be administered, but where it must be administered, with specific, um, instructions with regard to how a doctor is to administer it, how he's to . . . or she is to . . . instruct her patient, and so on and so forth. And again, I would expect that if this bill were to become law, a challenge would be made to that particular provision to determine whether it's consistent with the decision *Roe v. Wade* and *Doe v. Bolton*.

Watson: And is that because those cases said that the state can't unduly burden the exercise of that fundamental right?

Davis: That's correct.

Watson: And in your opinion, is that one of the restrictions that SB 5 does that may very well indeed unduly burden the exercise of that fundamental right recognized by the courts?

Davis: That's exactly right, and when the, when the Supreme Court recognized that right in *Roe v. Wade*, what they recognized was that any intrusion or alleged intrusion on that right would be subject to strict scrutiny by the court. And as you know as a lawyer, as I know as a lawyer, and other lawyers in the room know, that strict scrutiny is a very high standard. The state must demonstrate a compelling state interest in the laws that it's passing where there may be some constitutional infringements that might occur. And these are of course part of our questions with regard to SB 5 and its provisions: whether that strict scrutiny would allow, or even to find that there's a "compelling state interest." That's why I got so many questions. Senator Hegar and others with regard to the specific medical, empirical evidence that have demonstrated that the provisions of this bill actually are related to a "compelling state interest"—that somehow there is this interest that will be served in order to make them constitutionally viable under *Roe v. Wade* and subsequent decisions by the U.S. Supreme Court.

Watson: Part of my understanding, and I wanna, I wanna relate it to SB 5: You've talked about literal and practical limitations on the exercise of what has been recognized as a fundamental right, and you've talked about the strict scrutiny standard. Talk to me about in SB 5—part of what my understanding of *Roe v. Wade* and *Doe v. Bolton*, and correct me if I'm wrong, is that one of the things they said is that, that you can't unduly . . . the state can't unduly burden the exercise of that fundamental right with regulations that prohibit or substantially limit access to the means of effectuating the decision to have an abortion. Is that your understanding?

Davis: That's my understanding.

Watson: Take it to SB 5: is there anything in SB 5 that you believe is something we can point to that are regulations that prohibit or substantially limit access to the means of effectuating the decision for a woman to have an abortion, and exercise that fundamental right?

Davis: Yes, there are several things in SB 5 that I believe fall in that category. As I mentioned a moment ago, the requirement for an ambulatory surgical center . . . and in a moment, I have a book that describes what those rules are, what an ambulatory surgical center must provide, what the federal standards are, the current locations in Texas, and then also the overview of credentialing and physician privileges, because those are the key components of SB 5 that could be challenged under that particular provision that you just cited.

Watson: Explain that.

Davis: Well, arguments can be made, of course, that if that the ambulatory surgical center requirement is put in place, and if indeed it results in the closure of the vast majority of abortion clinics in the state of Texas, that could be deemed to limiting . . . if you'll say the language again . . .

Watson: Prohibit or substantially limit access to the means of effectuating the decision to have an abortion.

Davis: That could be ruled to substantially limit a woman's access. Also, what could be deemed to substantially limit a woman's access is the requirement that a provider, a, a physician provider of abortion services, must have admitting privileges in a hospital within 30 miles, because of that . . . of the fact that it may so severely decrease the number of physicians who are qualified under that law . . . not in reality, but under that law . . . who are qualified to provide services to women, that once again, to use that language, may . . .

Watson: . . . substantially limit access to the means of effectuating the decision.

Davis: Exactly. And then finally, um, taken together . . . and of course the state's laws have to be considered in a cumulative fashion . . . that SB 5 taken together with the sonogram law that passed in the last legislative session, may be deemed to have created constitutionally, um, suspect requirements that cannot meet those constitutional requirements. As you know, with that sonogram bill from the last legislative session, women now have a 24-hour waiting period after a sonogram before they can come back for their abortion procedure. If you add to that, for example, a provision in SB 5 that now requires that a woman who is going to receive an abortion through means of the abortion inducing drug, a woman who is to receive that now, under SB 5, would have to be given the drug . . . first of all, at an ambulatory surgical center, of which right now there are only five . . . and come back for her second dose 24 to 48 hours to receive that second dose. And again, we haven't heard any testimony, and I've asked questions about it and it certainly has been the topic of committee hearings, what it is about the woman taking, ingesting, that medicine, either orally or vaginally, in the presence of an ambulatory surgical center doctor, makes the provision of that abortion service somehow in the state's interest, somehow safer for her. And I think a constitutional challenge under that provision could be seen to be limiting her ability . . . [*Crosstalk*.]

Watson: Whether there's . . . your question was whether there's a compelling state interest to limit access so that she can effectuate that . . . her decision.

Davis: That's right.

Watson: Compare for me . . . 'cause you just mentioned the sonogram law, and I wanna talk about SB 5 as compared to the sonogram law. Were there changes made in the sonogram law in an effort to try to less limit access that aren't being made in SB 5?

Davis: That's right. In fact, SB 5 almost contradicts the changes that were put in place in the sonogram law.

Watson: Make sure I understand the changes that were made in the sonogram bill so that I'll understand what you say about what doesn't happen in SB 5 so that it contradicts.

Davis: In the sonogram what you may remember is Senator Estes, in order to secure his support on that bill, he was very insistent that women in the rural communities that he serves and that other members of this legislature serve, not have the burden of the 24-hour waiting period where the clinics were a far enough distance away from the woman's home that it would create a hardship on her to have to travel back to that clinic two days in a row.

Watson: So the argument would be that in order to not substantially limit access to the means of effectuating that woman's decision, there needed to be a change.

Davis: Correct.

Watson: I'm sorry, I interrupted you.

Davis: And you know, obviously that was made, um, to secure Senator Estes' comfort with the bill, and which he got there. I also believe though, that making that change made it legally less subject to challenge under the, the statutes that are in place today . . . the laws, the constitutional interpretative laws that are in place today. What happens in SB 5 that's different than that, is that in SB 5, the ambulatory surgical centers that exist in Texas today are in San Antonio, they're in Dallas, Austin, and Houston. And when you think about women needing to access those services, or desiring to access those services, living, once again, in some of the rural areas that Senator Estes represents, or perhaps that Senator Zaffirini represents, or that Senator Hinojosa represents or Senator Lucio represents . . . we know that if those become the only available abortion service centers in the state of Texas, women will have to travel, in some instances hundreds of miles in order to access abortion care services. And that might be subject to, and I believe it would be subject to, a challenge under the existing constitutional law as it relates to abortion.

Watson: And . . . and, um, you've indicated that there ought to be a compelling state interest . . . on that distance, I wanna make sure I understand your position . . . on the distance issue that we're talking about here, have you been satisfied that there is a compelling state interest to require clinics that currently can perform the termination of a pregnancy to go to an ambulatory . . . to go to the standard of an ambulatory surgical center . . . on, on, the the flip side of the coin, I guess, of limiting that access?

Davis: I do not believe that there has been any testimony, any empirical information, that has been provided on the senate floor, on the house floor, in the senate hearings both during the regular and the special session, in the house hearings both during the regular and the special session, that demonstrated some compelling state interest in this new provision that's being asked to pass into law in the state of Texas.

Watson: Now, I've asked you about these cases that serve as kind of the underpinnings for laws related to abortion and the constitutional right that a woman has to make these decisions. Um, I wanna ask you about in SB 5 another provision that, that I've heard you argue would limit access, and that is, uh, the 20-week provision. Are you familiar with any challenges that have been made in the United States to states that have created a 20-week provision like is in SB 5, where they've been challenged on the basis that they violate a woman's right to choose as protected by the United States constitution?

Davis: Yes, I am, and I think there have been four different states that have attempted, or have passed similar laws.

Watson: And I wanna be clear so that nobody has any question about, or . . . we're talking about the provision in SB 5?

Davis: That's correct

Watson: OK, I'm sorry.

Davis: And that provision in SB 5 is the same provision that's been passed into law in, I think, four other states, and has been the subject of litigation. Thus far, I don't think any court has found that that particular prohibition satisfies the constitutional requirements that have heretofore been set by the Supreme Court. And the reason that is prominently stated, or most often stated for that, is this issue of whether there truly is any scientific evidence that demonstrates fetal pain at that particular point in gestation. And that absent that compelling state interest, which might be found to be a legitimate one, because there hasn't been any scientific support to demonstrate that that has occurred, constitutionally, laws in other states that have attempted to do that have heretofore not been upheld.

Watson: Uh, something you had said earlier, either an answer to my question or somebody else's question, with regard to SB 5 and this 20-week provision, I want to make sure I understood. Help me understand, and I read some things from ACOG, the American Congress of Obstetricians and Gynecologists, uh, and, and, and other places, the difference between 20-weeks post-fertilization and 20-weeks gestation. Walk me through that as it applies to SB 5.

Davis: The concern that was raised, and I read a letter about it, I believe it was from TMA, it may have been from ACOG, a little while ago, it talked about the fact that the standard of determining the age of a fetus, the developmental age of a fetus, has always been based on prior menstrual cycle. And that is so because it's very difficult to determine the actual point of conception. For different women it's different, we ovulate at different times. But that seems to provide the most sound basis for making that determination. Under the provisions in SB 5 . . .

Watson: I'm sorry, if I might interrupt. The basis that is generally used as a sound basis for determining gestational time is last menstrual period?

Davis: Correct.

Watson: Alright. Sorry.

Davis: LMT, as it's referred to by doctors. And what's different about SB 5 is it asks instead for fertilization, the time of fertilization to become the operative time in which gestational age is measured. Now what the medical professionals say in the testimony they provided during committee and some of which I've read today, is that absent in-vitro fertilization, there really is no medically reliable way to determine what that date is. And in fact by using that date, it actually probably is overestimating fetal age, perhaps even significantly. So that a 20-week fetal age based on that point of reference . . .

Watson: Based upon fertilization.

Davis: Exactly. May be inaccurate and may be actually a gestational age that's only 18 weeks, for example.

Watson: OK. Is that one of the reasons, is it your understanding that that's one of the reasons that ACOG, which is the American Congress of Obstetricians and Gynecologists. I think I got that right, it may be American College, but ACOG has established that it's opposed to Senate Bill 5.

Davis: That's correct, that is one of their bases for opposition, among many.

Watson: Have you heard anything, either on the floor or in the hearings, that causes you to think that utilization, what SB 5 does, of the 20-weeks post-fertilization, is a more appropriate standard than what the American Congress of Obstetricians and Gynecologists are indicating ought to be any standard of use for determining gestational age, which is LMP?

Davis: I have not heard anything that leads me to believe that that is an incorrect, that the LMP is an incorrect way, and that that is a better way of determining gestational age.

Watson: Is there, in your mind, do you have any understanding as to why, in Senate Bill 5, there's an effort to utilize fertilization, 20-weeks post-fertilization, as opposed to utilizing LMP?

Davis: Well according to ACOG, their belief is that it is done in order to actually constrain even further, the limit upon which a woman could receive an abortion service, actually driving the gestational age, not even to 20 weeks, but even lower than 20 weeks, because they believe it would create a lower gestational age, and likely would be prohibiting women from having an abortion even as early as 18 weeks of pregnancy, rather than the current protection that exists under *Roe v. Wade* and *Doe v. Bolton*.

Watson: You mentioned earlier today, I think, that Senate Bill 5 is also opposed by the Texas Medical Association.

Davis: Correct.

Watson: And what is your understanding as to the reason the Texas Medical Association is opposing the passage of Senate Bill 5?

Davis: Their—the letter that they provided dealt in most part with the licensing of physicians that would be required under

Senate Bill 5. And that this requirement that a physician be licensed within a facility, a hospital, within 30 miles of the abortion facility is constraining the practice of medicine in a way that has not had a compelling interest demonstrated to, to, to prove why that's the case. They also have objected to the bill because of the, the piece that was originally in Senator Patrick's bill, in terms of how the abortion inducing drug is to be administered. And they believe that it is a tremendous, uh, stepping into the doctor patient relationship in a way that the legislature really has no business in treading upon, and can't demonstrate that they've intruded upon the patient doctor relationship in other instances, and why somehow in this particular arena they would, they would have this intrusion.

Watson: My memory is, in the debate on the Senate floor, with regard to SB 5, that, and I'm going to go to one of the reasons you said that you indicated you believed TMA had indicated the suppositions on Senate Bill 5, and one of those was the requirement of having admitting privileges a certain distance away, 30 miles away. My memory was, that in that debate, an amendment was offered, that that amendment said instead of the doctor needing to have privileges 30 miles away, we would codify an administrative code provision that would allow for that doctor to have a relationship with someone, another doctor, that had admitting privileges at a local hospital. Do you recall that?

Davis: I do recall that.

Watson: Now from the standpoint of, I know you wouldn't be able to speak for TMA on this, but if one of the objections of the leading physician organization in the state, is that you've created an undue restriction on access because physicians may not be able to have admitting privileges at, at a local hospital 30 miles away, one of the ways to solve for that would at least be to utilize something that's already in the administrative code, it's a rule that applies, and codify that where you would say, "We will be able to deal with emergencies under Senate Bill 5 by allowing that doctor to have a relationship with somebody at a local hospital." Is that correct?

Davis: That's correct.

Watson: So that would have at least been something, that if we're just talking about providing protection for women, and assuring that an appropriate standard of care is met, that would have been one way to assure that safety without unduly restricting a woman's access to making that decision.

Davis: That was the argument made at the introduction of that amendment, and I agree with the rationale behind that argument.

Watson: Another amendment that was offered, and let me ask you this question. In Senate Bill 5, which I think we would all agree, I don't think I'm going to get a point of order on asking this. Senate Bill 5 deals with abortions.

Davis: That's right, in fact I believe the subject line in the legislative list service where we typically look at our bills, the subject line on this bill says "abortion."

Watson: Um, and, and we've heard time and again that the reason to be for SB 5 is that we want to have safety for women, but we've also heard that it's to reduce the numbers of abortions. Have you heard that?

Davis: I'm sorry, can you repeat?

Watson: Sure, I'd be happy to. One of the reasons that we've heard that people support Senate Bill 5, is because they wanted to reduce the number of abortions.

Davis: That's right. Some people have indicated that.

Watson: And frankly, we would all like to reduce the number of abortions.

Davis: Yes, we would.

Watson: Is there anything in Senate Bill 5 that reduces, will help us reduce the number of unwanted pregnancies that could result in abortions?

Davis: In fact, I do not believe there is. And as you know,

Senator Watson, those were a pertinent part of our debates on Senate Bill 5. That we believed that while it, in the name of making better health services for women available, actually will decrease abortion services to women. We made arguments to decrease the need for abortion. We believed that the best way to decrease the need for abortion services was not through creating constitutional intrusions on women's rights to access those services, but instead to reduce the number of women who would be in demand for those services. Because there's certain things we could do at the state level to assist with that.

Watson: So for example, my memory is that amendments were offered on the floor to SB 5 that would have provided parents with notification about what their children were learning with regard to sex education in the schools.

Davis: That's correct, I believe you had two amendments that you offered in that regard, Senator.

Watson: And, and neither one of those amendments were taken on SB 5, so SB 5 doesn't have any provision in it that would help us reduce the number of unwanted pregnancies in the state.

Davis: That's correct.

Watson: And what's your understanding about where the state of Texas ranks in terms of the number of teen pregnancies?

Davis: I believe it's number two, I believe that's right. I know it's in the top three, but I believe it's number two in the country.

Watson: How about on second teen pregnancy?

Davis: I believe it's possibly even number one on second teen pregnancies, perhaps number two. We're right there in the top five, no question about it.

Watson: I want to go back to the idea that one of the reasons some have said, and I think, by the way, some of the members on the floor, um, legitimately want to increase that. I think all of us want to increase safety in any realm of healthcare that someone might be receiving.

Davis: That would be no question.

Watson: The argument has been made on SB 5, the reason we should be supportive of it is because it would provide greater public health, is that correct?

Davis: That's the argument that was made by Senator Hager, yes.

Watson: I'm looking at the ACOG letter, the letter that you referred to, which is the letter the American Congress of Obstetricians and Gynecologists in District 11 from Texas.

Davis: Yes.

Watson: I'm looking at page two.

Davis: Yes.

Watson: Down here at the bottom of the page, correct me if I'm wrong, one thing it says is that committee Senate Bill 5 requires additional standards that are unnecessary and unsupported by scientific evidence and then it indicates in that first bullet point, committee Senate Bill 5 does not promote the public health objective it claims to enhance, in fact it harms public health by restricting access to safe, legal and accessible abortion services. Now, I don't want to talk about the constitutional aspect of substantially limiting access to the means of effectuating the decision to have an abortion, that's protected by our United States Constitution, but let me ask you, what is ACOG talking about when it says it won't actually enhance safety, instead it will do the opposite?

Davis: Basically what it's saying is that it will do the opposite because women now will have limited access versus what they currently have in Texas today. And that that limited access actually will undermine women's health. It's not in this particular letter, Senator, I think ACOG wrote about four letters to us. It actually was not in the binder that I have either but I had it on the floor when we debated Senate Bill 5. And ACOG specifically, in the closing part of that letter, talked about the fact that they believed this will do harm to women's health in Texas. And they essentially cite to that period of time where women sought abortions in less safe conditions, and that they fear that with the limitation on where women can go to access these services, women, particularly poor women in rural communities will once again be driven to an unsafe environment where they seek abortion services. Interesting, Senator, uh statistic, and I know in one of these binders I have somewhere, there's this article about the fact that when you compare different countries and their abortions laws, the demand for abortions and the incidence of abortion does not go down even where the laws try to tightly confine it or prohibit it altogether. And when ACOG talks about that as it relates to Senate Bill 5, I think they understand all too well, much better than you or I, because this is the work that they do, they understand all too well that by changing the law in Texas and limiting women's access to where they will get safe legal abortions is not going to decrease the demand for abortion, but instead, it's going to push women into less safe circumstances where they'll seek it.

Watson: And it makes you worry, or let me ask you since I'm asking questions, does it make you worry that Senate Bill 5 won't limit abortions, it may just limit the legal ones.

Davis: And even further I would say it just may limit the safe ones.

Watson: Let me ask you about safety and unintended consequences of, of Senate Bill 5. Did ACOG make any reference to unintended consequences that would make the treatment of certain conditions, like ectopic pregnancies, more expensive?

Davis: Yeah.

Watson: Maybe you oughta—Could you explain that aspect of one of your concerns about Senate Bill 5?

Davis: Specifically, what ACOG said relative to the committee substitute for Senate Bill 5 was that it would have an unintended consequence by making the treatment of certain conditions more difficult and expensive. It says that ectopic pregnancies are frequently treated in outpatient facilities in physician office settings, and that SB 5 would prevent doctors from treating those cases as they normally would. I, I actually will share something very personal with you, I, I have experienced an ectopic pregnancy where I was able to be treated by my doctor in his office, and it's a very timely procedure, because . . .

Watson: Could you explain what it is?

Davis: Yes, an ectopic pregnancy is when the embryo begins to develop outside the uterus, typically in the fallopian tube. And if that is not immediately dealt with it can endanger the life of a woman if there is a rupture of the tube. Fortunately many women right now can go to their doctor and immediately upon discovery of that, rather than having to wait to be admitted to a hospital or an ambulatory surgical center, women can be treated for that ectopic pregnancy in that doctor's office.

Watson: Right there in the office.

Davis: Right there and right then, and the right then is the important part.

Watson: What does Senate Bill 5 do that changes that?

Davis: What Senate Bill 5 would do would be to require, according to ACOG, um, that those could no longer be provided in outpatient facilities, but instead that they would also have to be provided under ambulatory surgical center settings in order for the doctor who is providing that ectopic termination to be legal.

Watson: Thank you, Senator Davis. Thank you Mr. President.

Davis: Thank you. Members, I'd like to continue in reading some of the letters—

Dewhurst: You're recognized.

Davis: Thank you Mr. President, the letters that we've received on this particular bill. What folks have wanted to make sure that we consider as we are considering the passage of this bill and our discussion of this bill. [*Crosstalk.*]

Dewhurst: Senator Ellis, for what purpose do you rise, Sir?

Ellis: I have an inquiry, Mr. President.

Dewhurst: State your inquiry.

Ellis: Mr. President I want to ask you about rule 4.03. The last sub-section says, "no rule of the Senate prohibits repetitious remarks by a Senator if the remarks are germane to the matter under consideration." And that's from 76 in the journal, regular. Regular [*Unintelligible.*] 20, 1993. So my question is, I asked earlier about her reading the bill, I didn't get a clear answer, I think I could ask her because I think that is a bill I don't understand. But is it possible for me to ask Senator Davis to repeat the testimony, which we can all assume is germane because she gave that testimony earlier. At some point before midnight tonight can I ask her to go back and read those things that she read earlier from people who testified? Because I had to go off the floor a couple times and I did not really hear all of it. And I just wanted to make sure that that does not violate any Senate rule.

Dewhurst: Would you like [*unintelligible*] to get your copy?

Ellis: I have it here. Oh, a copy of her testimony? No sir, it's so much better when you have the human element involved. And slowly, preferably. I'm a slow learner Mr. President.

Davis: Mr. President I do still have the floor, I just want to make sure that we've established that I have not yielded the floor.

Dewhurst: Senator Davis, that's fine, you do have the floor. If you just bear with me just a moment I'm searching the [*unintelligible*].

Davis: Yes. [*Pause.*]

Dewhurst: Senator Ellis, your question is a hypothetical one. Since, since, since Senator Davis has been involved in answering questions I'm going to ask her to continue, and we'll make a ruling that the body, that the members, if they feel it's not germane they can raise points of order, but I'm not going to rule on a hypothetical question.

Ellis: Thank you, sir.

Dewhurst: Thank you. Senator Williams, for what purpose do you rise?

Williams: Mr. President, I'd like to raise a point of order that Senator Davis has violated a rule, 4.01, when she had Senator Ellis assist her by putting a back brace on during a pause a moment ago when we had a point of order raised and, uh, the members were at the dais.

Dewhurst: Would you all approach the podium? [*Extended pause.*]

Dewhurst: Senator Davis, I've been asked by a couple of the members whether during this discussion, whether you can sit down. And I understand—you might want to—

Davis: I'm fine.

Dewhurst: —but the parliamentarian has advised me that, that, you need to stay in the, in the debate—

Davis: I understand that rule and I'm prepared—

Dewhurst: I just wanted to share with you—

Davis: Thank you, Mr. President.

Zaffirini: Mr. President? Mr. President? For part of necessary inquiry related to your statement to Senator Davis just now.

Dewhurst: What is your inquiry?

Zaffirini: Related to Rule 4.06, Mr. President—it states, "When a member shall be called to order by the president or by a senator, the member shall sit down and not be allowed to speak, except to the point of order, until the question of order is decided. If the decision be in the member's favor, the member shall be at liberty to proceed. If otherwise, the member shall not proceed without leave of the senate." My question is, wouldn't Rule 4.06 allow Senator Davis or anyone else who is called to order or subject to the raising of a point of order, be required to speak during that time—be required sit during that time?

Dewhurst: Would you come forward, please? [*Pause.*] The point of order is overruled [*extended pause*]. Members, the point of order raised by Senator Williams deals with whether a member can assist another member during a filibuster. And the precedents in the rules clearly show that you can't leave anything on your desk—you've got to stay within a couple feet or three feet of the desk. During a filibuster, previous rulings have dealt with the comfort of a member during a filibuster. Now, while we've never seen a incident like this and a point of order raised like this, uh, I think this point of order addresses the issue of the comfort of a member and I think should be put to the body. So, I'm going to start off with—comment, I'm, I'm going to recognize—the Chair recognizes Senator Ellis to, to speak on the point of order.

Ellis: Thank you, Mr. President and members. I think the real issue here is whether or not this body respects the tradition of a filibuster or not. And here are the real rules of engagement. A majority of the members on this floor decide all of the power in this body. A majority of the members on this floor even decides who presides over the body. Anything that we do, any traditions that we have, can be trumped by 16 votes. Now, I have not been here as long as two other members on the floor. But I've been here for a very long time. As a staffer back in the mid-'70s, I remember when a distinguished Republican member of this body engaged in the longest filibuster that has been recorded in a State Legislature in the history of the country. Maybe one of the longest one-person filibusters in the history of not only State Legislatures but the Federal Legislature as well. Senator Bill Meier, from the Tarrant County area, I believe. At one point, back then, we didn't have the technology that we have today and he needed to take a break. But he was so passionate about the issue, whatever it was, as a young law student at LBJ School I can't remember what it was, but obviously, he was very passionate about it. At one point, he had to take a break and wouldn't leave the floor. And so, the members of the Senate—most of them were Democrats back then—stood around his desk. Now, I was in the gallery, but I clearly remember these same wooden trashcans that we have today. And some member of the opposing party was kind enough—dignified enough—respected this body and its traditions enough to organize his colleagues in both parties to stand around him in a circle, so that he could make the appropriate things that had to be put in place so he could continue his some 40-hour filibuster. Now, members, that's where we're really headed here. At any point, some member could make a motion, be recognized by a presiding officer and 16 votes or we don't have 31 here a majority of whatever is here—as long as we have a quorum—would decide you just shut off the filibuster. Now, I've seen that happen from time to time. But it has not been when it's been an issue that has been something that members felt this strongly about on either side of the political aisle or the philosophical aisle. I've seen that happen when somebody has not recognized the tradition of sending a letter in. Saying that, "I will filibuster," and a member would just get angry—two or three days in a row and decide, "Well, I'm going to filibuster that one and I'm going to filibuster that one." That has happened while many of you have been here on this floor. I won't call the names of the members, but I can remember at least two times that has happened to members. I can remember times in the past when members would pass some ice chips—someone would pass some Life Savers to someone. Usually, I might add, it would be someone who didn't agree with the position of the person who was filibustering. Members, that's really what this is about. What goes around tends to come around. If you don't respect the filibuster tradition—hey, I parrot that gaming legislation a number of years—Senator Corona has made progress with it as well. There will be members on this body who feel very strongly and adamantly against that legislation. And let me tell you, even if I'm carrying the bill, I would respect that member's right to use the tool of the filibuster to kill that bill or to stop that bill to make a point. So, members, that's really what it's all about. We've changed a lot of traditions in this body over the last several years. And I just want to encourage you, when you get ready to cast your vote, you're not going to reelected or elected based on this one vote. If you think this is going to hurt you that much if you vote your conscience, instead of what you're getting from your political analysts or staffers that may think they can tell you what the thing is you ought to do to make it safe—at some point you've got to decide—is winning everything? Is winning everything or do traditions in this body mean something to you? So, based on that, I would respectfully, as a member of this family—and it's a great family—on my, on my worst days around here, I can't think of a greater honor in my life than being one of the 31 members of the Texas Senate. And I want to ask you—I want to plead with you—don't destroy the few traditions that we've left in place in this body. Winning that one issue is not everything. Thank you.

Dewhurst: Thank you, Senator Ellis.

Zaffirini: Mr. President?

Dewhurst: Senator Zaffirini?

Zaffirini: Thank you, Mr. President.

Dewhurst: You're recognized.

Zaffirini: Thank you, Mr. President. Mr. President and members, I agree wholeheartedly with Senator Ellis and endorse every word that he said. In the 27 years that I have served in the Texas Senate and the years before that when I worked with Senator Wayne Connally, I saw firsthand the traditions of this Senate to support and to honor a person who was engaged in the filibuster, regardless of what side a senator was on. The question today focuses on specifically Article 4 of our rules—decorum and debate of members of the senate—members to address the president. Specifically, Senator Williams has raised an issue related to Rule 4.01. Allow me to read it to you. This is the rule and the only essence of this rule: "When a senator is about to speak in debate or to communicate any matter to the Senate, the member shall rise in his or her place and address the President of the Senate." That is the rule. There is no other part of this rule. Allow me to repeat it: "When a senator is about to speak in debate or to communicate any matter to the Senate, the member shall rise in his or her place and address the President of the Senate." Everything that Senator Davis has done is consistent with that rule. Now, granted, there is an editorial note. But it is only an editorial note. Allow me to read that to you: "A member who decides to speak on a pending question should address the chair and, having obtained recognition, may speak in an orderly and parliamentary way and subject to the rules of the Senate as long as he desires." Everything Senator Davis has done is consistent with that editorial note. Now, there are notes on two rulings. Those rulings were given 44 years ago in 1969. They are not rules. They are simply notes about another Lieutenant Governor's rules in 1969. Again, 44 years ago. The first note is this: "When a member has been recognized and is speaking on the notion to re-refer a bill, he must stand upright at his desk and may not lean thereon." Senator Davis has not leaned on her desk. And you know it because many of you are watching her every move—her every move. She has not leaned on her desk. The other note is this: "When a member has the floor and is speaking on the bill or resolution, he must stand upright at his desk and may not lean or sit on his desk or chair." Senator Davis has not leaned on her desk. She has not sat on her desk. She has not sat on her chair. And I might note, Mr. President, she's a woman. The note refers to "his desk," "his chair," so I would argue that this rule does not apply to Senator Davis. [*Laughter and applause.*] So, members, let's be literal about this. Let's be fair. Let's honor the tradition of the Texas Senate. And let's abide by the letter of the rules. Open your book. Look at your rules. Read it. And understand that everything Senator Davis has done is consistent with the rule of the Senate. Please read the rule, realize how specific it is, and honor this member and honor the tradition of the senate. Senator Davis, I applaud you for your understanding of the rules and for your being consistent with them in every way. Thank you for your leadership. Thank you, Mr. President and members.

Dewhurst: Senator Zaffirini. Senator Whitmire, you wanted to speak last. Is that what I heard? The Chair recognizes Senator Williams. Senator Whitmire wished to speak last, but—

Williams: Well, I think I brought the motion. I think I have the right to close. All I want to do is close. And then I'll have to make a motion to call for the vote. If that would please the chair.

Dewhurst: Senator Whitmire, I'm going to go ahead and recognize you, please.

Whitmire: Members, uh, it's kind of sad that we would normally have a senate caucus to resolve some of these matters. But we've allowed this issue and the politics surrounding today's deliberations to really kind of prevent us from having a senate caucus. Because normally we'd caucus, discuss procedural matters, scheduling, relationships—and we'd come out as the family that we're often referred to. But I haven't called a caucus because I didn't know what the endgame was, Senator Williams. Normally we have a caucus, we know what the considerations are and we decide that we're going to definitely come out with positive results and respect. But this week, you notice we haven't had a caucus. I've had a couple of people ask me—one, Senator Hegar—this would probably be an excellent opportunity for us to have a caucus. And I would actually entertain that matter. But we find ourselves considering this point of order, and I cannot do a better job than Senator Ellis reflecting on the traditions of the Senate. My good friend and second behind me in most seniority, Senator Zaffirini, talked about how we have assisted one another during debates. Senator Gonzalo Barrientos went 21 hours. People gave him ice cubes. I gave him some candy mints. The tradition of this body has been to assist another senator in being an effective senator representing his or her district and the people of Texas. We're very close to leaving that Senate tradition. Senator Williams, I have the highest respect for you. I've gone on and on this spring and this summer about the fine job you've done leading us and actually bringing us together producing a budget. I think, members, that we need to slow down right this moment and recognize what this very emotional issue is doing to this body. The politics of this issue—what it's doing to this body. And we must stop in our tracks and take a deep breath and look each other in the eye and remember the relationships—how we have gone to our—each other's children's services. How we have gone to each other's children's graduations. We weren't this tough on one another in trying to destroy this process during the days that we were in Albuquerque. Senator Duncan, you came to Albuquerque to talk to us to assist us in reaching a compromise and coming back to the state because of the damage it was doing to this body. We're worse off today than we were 35 days in Albuquerque—because then we were still respecting each other. I urge you to slow down. I can go back to when I got here in 1983 and tell you darn near every filibuster. Each one was unique. Each one was special. Even if you oppose the person's position, you were still kind to them. You still respected them as a Senator. You knew what they go through to get here. You know what it does to their families while they're gone for 140 days. Put back the face of the body that we work on on a daily basis. We'll be here until midnight tonight. We, we respect one another. And we've lost it. So let's slow down for a moment. Senator Davis, I've heard people on the opposing side grudgingly say, "She's doing an outstanding job." People of all persuasions in this body are respecting you now because you've been very statesman-like, doing something that I know most of us couldn't do. I think there's some resentment here because there are some members that either don't have the courage or the physical, or, or the capabilities to do it. There's admiration there. But what has happened, members, without going into the details of the issue before us, did Senator Ellis hand her a back brace or did not? Remember the other day when I was talking to you about an issue and I said, "Most often, on issues, and in my personal daily life, say, I put it to the greater good—the Greater

Good Test." So, I ask you to put this issue to the "Greater Good Test." What is the greater good? First of all, members, if she's found in violation, Senator Williams, it's going to be the second warning. It's not going to take her off the floor. So, you're not going to get the greater good of removing her from the floor. But isn't there a greater good of respecting a woman? Isn't it a greater good of respecting a colleague that asks someone to do something that she could have done for herself? Senator Ellis, you're the one we ought to be angry at. She didn't need your help. You didn't assist her. You made the mistake of being a gentleman and a colleague of handing her something from behind the brass rail. And then when she began to place it on her waist, you apparently made contact—Violation, Senator Ellis. Don't do it again. Members, the tradition of this body is you reach out and assist one another.

Whitmire: Members, the tradition of this body is you reach out and assist one another. We've had a great regular session. It's unfortunate that we find ourselves in a special. It's unfortunate that we find ourselves then with an emotional issue, and this is before, Senator Williams, I rest, I would say: members, separate the emotion of the issue, which will be resolved sooner than later. And quite frankly, members, there's a right way to do something and there's a wrong way. I think you know you have the votes in a special session to pass this piece of legislation, which I oppose. If you don't complete it tonight, it's none of our fault that it was placed in the call 2 weeks into the special, that the House spent more time maybe than was anticipated. If we don't finish it tonight, we can start back at the call of the governor's message, and ultimately you probably have the votes, unfortunately, to pass this. So, this is not an up or down position on this issue, which is yet to be resolved; this is about the dignity of the body, the integrity of the body, and I would ask you, don't let this be a partisan vote. Don't let this be a vote whether you're for or against Senate Bill 5. Let this be a vote on the respect, the tradition of this body, and quite frankly . . . I will close by saying when I sit down, regardless of how this vote is resolved, can we not commit ourselves to going through the remainder of these considerations without personal attacks. Senator Nichols, can we just agree to let her finish her filibuster; it is a legislative procedure that historically in this body separates us from other bodies. That's why we're not, in all due respect, the Texas House of Representatives. They raise points of orders on each other regularly. We allow people to file bills after the constitutional deadline. We try to assist each other in being effective representatives of our districts. Some eight 800,000 plus people depend on each and every one of us. So I will say, Mr. President, under oath if necessary; I have seen the tradition of this body allow what took place on that side of the chamber, where Senator Ellis assisted by giving her something that she could do herself. She did not lean, she did not sit, she's been an outstanding state senator that in the tradition of this body if we even disagree with her, we oughtta respect her convictions and her opportunity to represent her district and her point of view. Members, do what is the greater good in respecting a colleague, and let's finish this debate tonight honorably.

Dewhurst: Senator Whitmire, I don't think anyone's questioning their respect, and I'm not gonna get into a dialogue. I think we all respect Senator Davis, and we . . . I agree she's doing a good job although I disagree with her, but she's . . . I think she's doing a good job. Um . . . Senator Lucio, for what purpose do you rise?

Lucio: Very briefly to make a comment, Mr. President.

Dewhurst: You're not recognized; we had three comments by, by . . . [Pause.]

Lucio: Thank you, Mr. President. [Crosstalk.]

Dewhurst: I'll recognize you for some brief comments.

Lucio: Very briefly, I came in a couple of months after my good friend, Senator Ellis. I too have seen many things happen on this senate floor for close to 23 years now. I'm fourth in seniority behind the Dean, Senator Zaffirini, and Senator Ellis. I too had a bill filibustered my first year here, and we were able to pass that bill over the objections of Senator Carlos Truan, the late Carlos Truan . . . I gave him a cough drop during the process 'cause I felt sorry for my colleague, and I respected him, and he had the right to speak out against my bill. I did exactly what Senator Ellis stated a little while ago. So I just wanna go on record . . . I want this bill to pass, but yet I stand before you to tell you that Senator Davis does have the right to oppose this bill until she drops. And I don't think that'd be before twelve. And I, I just wanna say this, that we have an opportunity of a lifetime to be able to show not only Texas, but the whole country, what we're all about, and let's do it right. Thank you.

Dewhurst: The Chair recognizes Senator Williams.

Williams: Thank you, Mr. President. Members, there's been a lot of things said here, and I'm just gonna make a few comments; we've all been here a long time. The first thing I would say is that I have enormous respect for Senator Davis, she is my desk mate, she sits right behind me, we chat frequently, we agree on very little, but we, we are on friendly terms and I've included her in many meetings in the finance committee and given her opportunities to ask question extensively . . . the implication that I have anything but the deepest respect for her is, frankly, out of bounds. And what I would further say is that I have tremendous respect for the traditions of this senate. And I wanna be clear about what my objection is here. The tradition and the rules that we have, and I would encourage you to read rule 4.01 and all the notes of the ruling, some of which have been conveniently omitted by my colleagues as they read them aloud to all of us; I would encourage you to read all of those. And what I would say is that it's very clear to me, and it was made clear to me when I came to the senate, and in the filibusters that I have witnessed during the twelve years that I've been here—the six regular sessions and so many special sessions I can't count 'em anymore—ah, that a filibuster is an endurance contest, and it's to be made unaided and unassisted. And that's been made very clear to me since the very beginning. And what my objection relates to is not the fact that Senator Davis is wearing a back brace. I'm wearing orthotics and tennis shoes because my back bothers me and my feet are bothering me, too. I don't object to that at all. But the tradition of this filibuster in the senate has always been that you had to do it on your own. And, and, Senator Ellis, you're well aware of that, I believe, because I was frankly surprised that you said you didn't help her put it on and there's a picture on Twitter right now of you helping her put it on . . . when we were at the front dais you said, no, I just handed it to her. And there's a picture of you putting it around her waist, just as I said. And so frankly I'm surprised at the implication here that things were just handed across the rail and it was like a piece of paper, and that's not true . . . that's not what happened. And so I wanna be clear that I have enormous respect for Senator Davis, I respect her right to filibuster, and I think that it is an important tradition that I hope we will maintain in this body. And part of that tradition is that the rules clearly state, ah, under what circumstances you can filibuster, and if three points of order are called—and we've had clarification on this from Senator West—if three points of order are called, then you cannot continue your filibuster. And that further points to what my point is, that it is an endurance contest. And so I respectfully, uh, ask that you would vote with me on this, and Mr. President, uh, I would move that we . . . Mr. President, I think you've indicated that you'd like for the body to vote on this, and I would like to make the appropriate motion to do so.

Dewhurst: You are recognized.

Williams: I move the question on the point of order?

Dewhurst: Members, the issue before us is whether or not the point of order raised by Senator Williams be sustained. The Secretary will call the roll. [*Pause.*] A vote yes is to sustain the point of order, no is to not sustain the . . .

Secretary: Birdwell, Campbell, Corona, Davis, Deuell, Duncan, Ellis, Eltife, Estes, Fraser, Garcia, Hancock, Hegar, Hinjosa, Huffman, Lucio, Nelson, Nichols, Patrick, Paxton, Rodriguez,

Schwertner, Seliger, Taylor, Uresti, Van de Putte, Watson, West, Whitmire, Williams, Zaffirini.

Dewhurst: Members, seventeen ayes and eleven nays, the point of order is sustained. The chair recognizes Senator West, for what purpose?

West: Will this ruling be . . . would a motion be in order to spread this ruling on the, uh, on the journal?

Dewhurst: I'm sorry, say again, Sir.

West: In terms of making sure that this ruling be reduced to writing and be spread upon the journal.

Dewhurst: Yes, I . . . members, Senator West moves to . . . to put the exchange that has occurred on this ruling in the journal. Is there an objection from any member? Chair has no objection, it's so ordered.

West: Parliamentary inquiry.

Dewhurst: State your . . . your inquiry.

West: In terms of . . . and I know I can go look at these rules . . . in terms of the rules that govern appeals, an appeal of the Chair's ruling . . .

Dewhurst: Right.

West: What are those rule numbers, and what's the process? [*Pause.*] What rules govern appeals of the Chair's decision, and what is the process? [*Extended pause.*]

Dewhurst: Senator West, on an appeal by ruling by the Chair . . . by, in this case, the President, um, it can be made by any member, and then it's put to a vote of the body.

West: Is it immediately put to a vote at that time, or is there a process that's put in place? Do you have to go through a process before you can put it to the vote?

Dewhurst: Senator West, the members could debate . . . there could be some debate on the point of order, as we just did, but then it's put to a vote of the body.

West: OK, thank you.

Dewhurst: Senator Watson, for what purpose?

Watson: Parliamentary inquiry.

Dewhurst: State your inquiry, sir.

Watson: The ruling that was just made with regard to Senator Williams' point of order; what is the effect of that ruling?

Dewhurst: The effect that it's the second warning to Senator Davis. The first warning, many hours ago, was on germaneness; this is the second warning. If there's a third warning, then that would go to the vote of the body to make a decision as to whether or not the filibuster continues.

Watson: Parliamentary inquiry.

Dewhurst: State your inquiry, Sir.

Watson: And I think I know the answer based upon the practice we've been following here tonight, but I wanna make sure for the rest of the evening. A member of the senate rising with a parliamentary inquiry does not cause Senator Davis to yield the floor to that person.

Dewhurst: That is correct.

Watson: Thank you, Mr. President.

Dewhurst: Thank you, Senator Watson. Senator Whitmire, for what purpose?

Whitmire: Parliamentary inquiry. Following Senator Watson's questioning: so there have been a finding of two violations, sustained point of orders, at this point.

Dewhurst: That is correct.

Whitmire: So if there is another then you'll submit the question to the body as to whether the debate . . . I mean the filibuster . . . shall continue?

Dewhurst: Yes, that is correct.

Whitmire: Could the Parliamentarian maybe advise Senator Davis, certainly myself, how would be the best way . . . first of all, there was a ruling earlier that she's not responsible if someone asks her a non-germane question . . .

Dewhurst: That is exactly right, and she was not called . . . there's been no warning on Senator Davis for a non-germane question by another member.

Whitmire: So as she continues her filibuster and answering questions, I'd assume the burden is on her to make absolutely certain that every time she says something that it's germane, because we know that there are members looking for the opportunity for that third point of order. Can this Parliamentarian, or even you, Mr. President, as our leader, is there any way you could advise Senator Davis or those asking questions to make certain that they're germane? I mean, if, if in fact we want this process to go forward, how could we prevent, on behalf of the senate, from having someone raise that third point of order?

Dewhurst: By focusing the questions and the answers by Senator Davis on Senate Bill 5, the body of the legislation, the different parts of it, and focusing both questions and answers on the bill before us, which is Senate Bill 5.

Whitmire: OK, being very positive, that that's going to occur . . .

Dewhurst: Senator Whitmire, would you pause just for a moment? [*Pause.*] The Parliamentarian wanted me to make clear, and I thought I had, that the warning to Senator Watson has no impact whatsoever, and is not counted in . . . towards Senator Davis.

Whitmire: But this last vote was the second point of order.

Dewhurst: Correct.

Whitmire: And if I understood from your answer a moment ago, the next one will submit the question to the body as to whether to continue the filibuster. Which is why I'm trying to be as cautious as I can with the leadership, Senator Davis, and the members, that if everyone makes certain that their questions and commentary is germane, there's no reason why this filibuster should not be allowed to continue to conclusion, assuming Senator Davis' strength, capabilities, and motivation, and . . . I know she wants to, so if everything is germane, uh, this leads to my next question. Assuming she's able to go forward, which I'm positive . . . [Crosstalk.] . . . what is this leadership's plan to do with SDR 2 and Senate Bill 23?

Dewhurst: Senator Whitmire, so as that we don't have another filibuster going right now . . . it's clear that the body, Republicans and Democrats, are observing the tradition of the senate having a filibuster. Having said that, it's also clear that from the will of the majority of the senators that there's a . . . um . . . that strict enforcement should be maintained, period. And you know that better than I do.

Whitmire: And I think that's fair to put every member present, certainly Senator Davis on notice . . . strict enforcement, that means the questions and the answers and any discussion during a filibuster is gonna be watched very carefully, 'cause we understand the motivation by those that are raising the point of orders. So, we're all on notice, and there's no reason, though, with that notice that we shouldn't be able to go forward . . . [Crosstalk.]

Dewhurst: Senator Whitmire . . . yes, and thank you very much. I'm gonna recognize Senator Davis to continue.

Zaffirini: Mr. President? Mr. President?

Dewhurst: Senator Zaffirini, for what purpose . . .

Zaffirini: Parliamentary inquiry, Mr. President.

Dewhurst: State your inquiry.

Zaffirini: Thank you. To follow up on Senator Whitmire's

line of questioning, suppose that an unfriendly senator, and I mean unfriendly to the issue that Senator Davis is promulgating . . . suppose that an unfriendly senator asks a question that is not germane, and asks perhaps a series of questions that are not germane, and Senator Davis politely answers the question. Would she be held responsible for answering a question that is not germane?

[*Pause.*]

Dewhurst: Senator Zaffirini, I've addressed that before in my comments about Senator Watson, in which . . . so that, that a question by a senator that's not germane to Senator Davis, is not counted as a warning.

Zaffirini: Even if she answers?

Dewhurst: Even if she answers.

Zaffirini: Thank you, Mr. President.

Dewhurst: But the next point of order that is sustained, I have to put it to the body for a decision.

Zaffirini: Thank you.

Dewhurst: The Chair recognizes Senator Davis.

Davis: Thank you, Mr. President. I want to continue by reading the portion of the bill as it came back over from the House. As you know, members, when we passed this bill out of the Senate, we passed it without the prohibition of abortion at or after 20 weeks post-fertilization. So first I'm going to read that section of the bill, and then I'm going to read some medical information with regard to the 20-week provision, and whether indeed the findings of the bill that support the inclusion of this sub-chapter are indeed in keeping with scientific research. The bill's section where this can be found is on page three of the House amendments to committee substitutes to Senate Bill 5 . . . on page 3 of the bill. Under Subchapter C, the title of the subchapter is "Abortion Prohibited at or After 20 Weeks Post-fertilization." Section 171.041, Short Title: This subchapter may be cited as the "Pre-born Pain Act."

Section 171.042 definitions: In this subchapter, post-fertilization age means the age of the unborn child as calculated from the fusion of a human spermatozoa with a human ovum. Subchapter . . . or subsection 2: severe fetal abnormality has the meaning assigned by section 285.202. Section 171.043—Determination of post-fertilization age required. Except as otherwise provided by section 171.046—a physician may not perform or induce, or attempt to perform or induce, an abortion without, prior to the procedure, number 1: making a determination of the probable post-fertilization age of the unborn child, or number 2: possessing and relying on a determination of the probable post-fertilization age of the unborn child made by another physician. Section 171.044— Abortion of unborn child of 20 or more weeks post-fertilization age prohibited. Except as otherwise provided by Section 171.046, a person may not perform or induce, or attempt to perform or induce, an abortion on a woman if it has been determined by the physician performing, inducing, or attempting to perform or induce the abortion, or by another physician on whose determination that physician relies, that the probable post-fertilization age of the unborn child is 20 or more weeks. Section 171.045— Method of abortion. Subsection A–This section applies only to an abortion authorized under Section 171.046, subsection A–1 or 2, in which, 1: the probable post-fertilization age of the unborn child is 20 or more weeks, or 2: the probable post-fertilization age of the unborn child has not been determined, but could reasonably be 20 or more weeks. Subsection B—Except as otherwise provided by Section 171.046, subsection A-3, a physician performing an abortion under subsection A shall terminate the pregnancy in the manner that in the physician's reasonable medical judgment, provides the best opportunity for the unborn child to survive. Section 171.046 lays out the exceptions. A: The prohibitions and requirements under Sections 171.043, 171.044, and 171.045b do not apply to an abortion performed if there exists a condition that, in a physician's reasonable medical judgment, so complicates the medical condition of the woman, that to avert the woman's death or a serious risk of substantial and irreversible physical impairment of a major bodily function, other than a psychological condition, it necessitates as applicable, 1: the immediate abortion of a pregnancy without the delay necessary to determine the probable post-fertilization age of the unborn child; 2: the abortion of her pregnancy, even though the post-fertilization age of the unborn child is 20 or more weeks; or 3: the use of a method of abortion other than a method described by Section 171.045b. Subsection B—A physician may not take an action authorized under Subsection A if the risk of death or a substantial and irreversible physical impairment of a major bodily function arises from a claim or diagnosis that the woman will engage in conduct that may result in her death, or in substantial and irreversible physical impairment of a major bodily function. Subsection C—The prohibitions and requirements under Sections 171.043, 171.044, and 171.045b do not apply to an abortion performed on an unborn child who has a severe fetal abnormality. Section 171.047 provides for protection of privacy in court proceedings. Subsection A—Except as otherwise provided by this section, in a civil or criminal proceeding or action involving an act prohibited under this subchapter, the identity of a woman on whom an abortion has been performed or induced, or attempted to be performed or induced, is not subject to public disclosure if the woman does not give consent to disclosure. Unless the court makes a ruling under Subsection C to allow disclosure of the woman's identity, the court shall issue orders to the parties, witnesses, and counsel, and shall direct the sealing of the record and exclusion of individuals from courtrooms or hearing rooms to the extent necessary to protect the woman's identity from public disclosure. A court may order the disclosure of information that is confidential under this section if a motion is filed with the court requesting release of the information and a hearing on that request. Notice of the hearing is served on each interested party, and the court determines after the hearing and an in-camera review, that disclosure is essential to the administration of justice and there is no reasonable alternative to disclosure.

Dewhurst: Excuse me for a second, Senator Davis. Senator Deuell, were you rising?

Senator Deuell: I have a question for the, for Senator Davis, but if she's just gonna read that section I'll wait till she's finished; I wasn't gonna rise until then.

Dewhurst: All right, I'll recognize you in a few minutes.

Deuell: Is that her intent, to . . .

Davis: My intent, Senator Deuell, is to finish reading the subsection as it relates to the Fetal Pain Bill.

Deuell: OK, I'll let you . . . it'd be OK with me to let her finish that, then I have some questions if she'd yield for that.

Dewhurst: Senator Davis has the floor.

Davis: Section 171.048—Construction of Subchapter A. This Subchapter shall be construed as a matter of state law, to be enforceable up to but no further than the maximum possible extent consistent with federal constitutional requirements, even if that construction is not readily apparent, and such constructions are authorized only to the extent necessary to save the Subchapter from judicial invalidation. Judicial reformation of statutory language is explicitly authorized only to the extent necessary to save the statutory provision from invalidity. Subsection B—If any court determines that a provision of this Subchapter is unconstitutionally vague, the court shall interpret the provision as a matter of state law to avoid the vagueness problem, and shall enforce the provision to the maximum possible extent. If a federal court finds any provision of this Subchapter, or its application to any person, group of persons or circumstances to be unconstitutionally vague and declines to impose the saving constructions described by the subsection. The Supreme Court of Texas shall provide an authoritative construction of the objectionable statutory provision that avoids the Constitutional problem while enforcing the statutes restrictions to the maximum possible extent, and shall agree to answer any questions certified from a Federal Appellate Court regarding the statute. Subsection C—A state executive or an administrative official may not decline to enforce this subchapter or adopt a construction of this subchapter in a way that narrows its applicability, based on the official's own beliefs about what the State or Federal Constitution requires, unless the official is enjoined by State or Federal Court from enforcing the subchapter. Subsection D—This subchapter may not be construed to authorize the prosecution of, or cause of action to be brought against a woman on whom an abortion is performed, or induced, or attempted to be performed, or induced in violation of this subchapter.

Now, that of course is the entirety of the provision, um, that deals with fetal pain in the 20-week prohibition, with the exception of the introduction portion of the bill. And it states that the findings indicate, doesn't say whose findings at one point in time, it said, "The legislature finds that" and I think Senator Zaffirini objected to that in committee that the legislature as a body had made no such findings that she was aware of, and it was changed. The language was changed, so now it simply says, "The findings indicate that the State has a compelling state-interest in protecting the lives of unborn children from the stage at which substantial medical evidence indicates that these children are capable of feeling pain." And what I have here, members, is a study specific to that particular issue and whether, uh, there is the ability, or scientific evidence that demonstrates the ability regarding fetal pain. It's a key provision of this bill and it's a key provision of the state's stated interest in why passage of a 20-week ban would be allowed. I have here a clinical review dated August 24th through the 31st 2005, published in something called *Clinician's Corner*, the authors being Susan J. Lee J.D., Henry J. Peter Rolfson M.D., Elenor A. Dre M.D. E.D.M., John Collin Partridge M.D. MPH, and Mark A. Rosen M.D. The affiliations of these authors, Ms. Lee, the School of Medicine; Dr. Rolfson, Department of Anatomy, and WM Tech Foundation of Integrative Neuroscience; Doctors Dre and Rosen, Departments of the Obstetrics, Gynecology and Reproductive Services; Dr. Partridge, Pediatrics; Dr. Rosen, Anesthesia and Peri-Operative care and also the University of California, San Francisco. The context in the abstract is that proposed Federal

Legislation would require physicians to inform women seeking abortions at 20 or more weeks after fertilization, that the fetus feels pain, and to offer anesthesia administered directly to the fetus. Now, of course, this would simply address an issue where women were being told that they are going to submit a fetus to pain if undergoing an abortion. And it analyzes whether fetal pain actually has been medically demonstrated again, as in, as is the context in the defense of this provision in Senate Bill 5. For evidence acquisition, there was a systematic search conducted by the authors of PubMed for English language articles focusing on human studies related to fetal pain, anesthesia and analgesia. Included articles studied fetuses of less than 30 weeks gestational age or specifically addressed fetal pain for perception or no perception. Articles were reviewed for additional references. The search was performed without date limitations and was current as of June of '05. The evidence synthesis here provides that pain perception requires conscious recognition or awareness of a noxious stimulants. Neither withdrawal reflexes nor hormonal stress responses to invasive procedures prove the existence of fetal pain, because they can be elicited by non-painful stimuli and occur without conscious cortical processing. Fetal awareness of noxious stimuli requires functional thalama-cortical connections. Thalamacortical fibers begin appearing between 23 to 30 weeks gestational age while electroenceph-alography suggests the capacity for functional pain perception in preterm neonates probably does not exist before 29 or 30 weeks. For fetal surgery, women may receive general anesthesia and/or analgesics intended for placental transfer and corential opioids may be administered to the fetus under direct or sono-graphic visualization. In these circumstances, administration of anesthesia and analgesia serves purposes unrelated to reduction of fetal pain, including inhibition of fetal movement, preven-tion of fetal hormonal stress responses, and induction of uterine atenine. The conclusion from the abstract found that evidence regarding the capacity for fetal pain is limited, but indicates that fetal the perception for pain is unlikely before the third-tri-mester. Little or no evidence address the effectiveness of direct fetal anesthetic or analgesic techniques. Similarly limited or no data exists on the safety of such techniques for pregnant women in the context of abortion. Anesthetic techniques currently used during fetal surgery are not directly applicable to abortion procedures. Over the last several years many states including California, Kentucky, Minnesota, Montana, New York, Oregon, and Virginia, have considered legislation requiring physicians to inform women seeking abortion that the fetus feels pain and to offer fetal anesthesia. This year, Arkansas and Georgia enacted such statutes and of course, now, under this bill, the State of Texas would not only be enacting a statute that would, uh, require anesthesia, in fact it wouldn't require that at all, it would absolutely prohibit abortion at 20 weeks, using as the basis for that new state regulation, the existence of fetal pain and of course, in the bill's language, "scientific evidence," that demonstrates that.

According to these authors, currently Congress is considering legislation requiring physicians to inform women seeking abortions 20 or more weeks after fertilization, i.e. 22 weeks gestational age, that the fetus has physical structures necessary to experience pain as evidenced by drawing away from surgical instruments. The physician must also offer anesthesia or analgesia administered directly to the fetus. Physicians who do not comply may be subjected to substantial fines, license revocation, and civil suits for punitive damages. Although that national legislation that they're talking about would not affect most U.S. abortions, because only 1.4% are performed at or after 21 weeks of gestational age, this legislation raises important scientific, clinical, ethical and policy issues. And of course, members, the legislation before us raises the same clinical, ethical and policy issues. And the important question is, "When does a fetus have the functional capacity to feel pain?" If we're going to justify the inclusion of a 20-week abortion ban in this bill, it's important that we answer that question. As a first step in answering it, the authors reviewed the literature on fetal pain and fetal anesthesia and analgesia. Now their evidence acquisition, in order to reach their findings, consisted of the following: They reviewed English language articles involving human participants, and searched PubMed for articles on fetal pain; they found 16 articles; articles on fetal anesthesia, they found 6 articles; article on fetal analgesia, they found 3 articles; fetus and anesthesia or analgesia, they found 1,239 articles; medical subject headings using the terms, "analgesics" "administration" and "dosage" and "fetus," they found 44 articles; M.E.S.H., and anesthesia, administration, and dosage, and fetus, they found zero articles in that. Searching under neurodevelopment or development or anatomy and fetus or fetal and pain or no susception or noxious they found 306 articles. Searching under terms thalamocortical or thalamus or cortex and fetus or fetal and pain or no susception or noxious they found 13 articles. Searching under terms, "electroencephalog" or "EEG O-Revoked Potential" and "Fetus" or "Fetal" or "premature" or "premature neonatal" or "premature infant" or "preterm neonatal" or "preterm infant" and "pain" or "noxious consciousness" they found 7 articles. The search was performed without date limitations and was current as of the date of this article. And from those search results, they excluded articles that did not study fetuses of less than 30 weeks gestational age or did not specifically address fetal pain perception or no susception. For a focus on topics addressed by earlier review articles on fetal pain, anesthesia and analgesia, articles were reviewed for additional references. The synthesis of that evidence, uh, in this journal entry was that pain is a subjective sensory and emotional experience that requires consciousness to permit recognition of a stimulus as unpleasant. Although pain is commonly associated with physical noxious stimuli, such as when one suffers a wound, pain is fundamentally a psychological construct that may exist even in the absence of physical stimuli, as seen in phantom limb pain. The psychological nature of pain also distinguishes it from no susception, which involves physical activation of no-susceptic pathways, without the subjective emotional experience of pain. For example, no susception without pain exists below the level of a spinal cord lesion where reflex withdrawal from a noxious stimulus occurs without conscious perception of pain. And they have a diagram to indicate what they're talking about there. And they find that because pain is a psychological construct with emotional content, the experience of pain is modulated by changing emotional input, and may need to be learned through life experience. Regardless of whether the emotion content of pain is acquired, the psychological nature of pain presupposes the presence of functional thalamcortical circuitry required for conscious perception as discussed below. No susception may be characterized by reflex movement in response to a noxious stimulus without cortical involvement or conscious pain perception. No susception involves peripheral sensory receptors, whose afferent fiber synapse in the spinal cord on interneurons which synapse on motor neurons that also reside in the spinal cord. These motor neurons trigger muscle contractions, causing limb reflection away from a stimulus. In contrast, pain perception requires cortical recognition of the stimulus as unpleasant. Peripheral sensory receptor efferent synapse on spinal cord neurons, the axons of which project to the thalamus, which sends efferents to the cerebral cortex. By activating any number of cortical regions, sensory receptors in spinal cord synapses required for no susception develop earlier than the thalamcortical pathways required for conscious perception of pain.

Now, once again, I refer to the section of the bill:

"The State has a compelling State interesting in protecting the lives of unborn children from the stage at which substantial medical evidence indicates that these children are capable of feeling pain."

The abstract that I just read you refutes that. There are other articles that refute that as well. I want to go to the bill analysis of the bill and read that section in the bill analysis.

Deuell: Mr. President. I've been waiting; I think this may be a good time for me to ask questions, if Senator Davis would allow me to do so without yielding the floor?

Davis: Not at this time, Mr. President.

Dewhurst: Do you have an idea of how long you would want to wait?

Davis: I'm not sure at this point.

Dewhurst: Would you hold for a moment? [*Pause.*] Senator Davis has the floor; I'll come back to you. Could you hold just for a moment?

Deuell: Yes sir.

Dewhurst: Thanks.

Davis: Thank you, Mr. President. I'm going to read the bill analysis and there of course is a section here that deals with the fetal pain issue as well. This is the bill analysis prepared on June the 14th, 2013 to the substituted committee report, the Committee Substitute to Senate Bill 5, prepared by the Senate Research Center. Under the section about the authors sponsored statement of intent, it states that, "At 20 weeks post-fertilization, scientific evidence suggests that preborn children are capable of feeling pain as all the neuroreceptors for pain are in place and functioning. Myriad peer reviewed studies have found anatomical, behavioral, and physiological evidence that the developing preborn child is capable of experiencing pain by 20 weeks post fertilization." A 2007 study by the Department of Obstetrics and Gynecology at the University of Arkansas for Medical Science states that, "fetuses undergoing intrauterine invasive procedures definitively illustrative of pain signaling were reported to show coordinated responses signaling the avoidance of tissue injury. Preborn pain laws similar to this legislation have been passed in other states." But this doesn't indicate, of course is that those have been subject to challenge and those challenges have been, at this point, successful. Committee Substitute to Senate Bill 5 establishes a separate and independent compelling State interest in protecting the lives of the unborn children from the State, at which the medical evidence indicates they are capable of feeling pain. Mifeprex RU486 was approved by the United States Food and Drug Administration, FDA, for use by pregnant women wishing to terminate a pregnancy for up to 49 days gestation only. The drug has no other approved indication for use during pregnancy. The RU486 label instructs that tablets are intended for oral administration only, and should be administered only in a clinic, medical office or hospital, and by or under the supervision of a physician able to assess the gestational age of an embryo and to diagnose ectopic pregnancies. Abortion inducing drugs pose substantial risks to women and these risks are magnified when the drugs are misused. The purpose of Committee Substitute to Senate Bill 5 is to protect the health and welfare of women considering a drug-induced abortion. It ensures physicians providing drug-induced abortions are only doing so in the way in which the FDA tested and approved the abortion inducing drug. And of course, we had a tremendous amount of testimony during the debate on this bill about that particular provision and about whether that actually is in keeping with medical evidence that's been learned by practicing physicians with the use of this drug. Senator Vanderpute, of course, made a compelling as a pharmacist about the fact that, were the provisions of this bill to go into law as they're discussed here in the bill analysis, it actually controverts the medical practice, the current medical practice and use of that drug for purposes of medical abortion. And it does that, because over time, what doctors who administered this drug have found, is that women who have been administered the drug, number one, need far lower dosage than what the FDA had originally put in place, and also number two, that using the drug, especially on the second day, through vaginal insertion versus oral administration, actually produced much better and safer outcomes for the patients. As a consequence of that, we worked on making changes to that, but this amendment that came over from the House, I do not believe included the amendments that were made, to try to acknowledge and put into place Senator's Vanderpute's concerns that she justifiably raised with regard to that particular provision of the bill. Committee Substitute to Senate Bill 5 according to the bill analysis requires that Texas abortion providers meet the basic standards described by the manufacturer of RU486 and the FDA, and again those are in direct contradiction to the use of the drug today, that medical practitioners have determined to be safest for women. And of course, it begs the question that we've talked about earlier today, about legislators stepping into the role of medical providers and making decisions about administrations of drugs to women under the argument that doing it in this particular manner is safer when, in fact, practicing medical professionals have found otherwise. The concern being, that through this legislation, we actually are creating a less healthy climate for women who might take this drug than there would be, um, under the ways that physicians are currently administering it. Committee Substitute to Senate Bill 5 also requires that the woman receive the name and telephone number of the physician or other healthcare other personnel who will handle emergencies that arise from the use of the abortion inducing drug. And finally, the physician must provide a written report of adverse events to the FDA Medwatch Reporting System. Now members, I firmly believe, that had those been the sole provisions of this bill, there would have been uniform support, both of which provide ways I think we would all find common agreement, create a safer climate for women who are undergoing abortion. One, that the woman as she leave the abortion clinic, I do believe that this is the practice today, but it certainly doesn't hurt to assure that it is more than just a practice, that is actually a requirement, that as women leave a facility, they be given the name and telephone number of the physician or other healthcare personnel who will handle emergencies that arise from the use of the abortion inducing drug. And that makes sense of course. And that the physician should give a report on adverse events to the FDA Medwatch Reporting System makes excellent sense as well.

Deuell: Mr. President?

Dewhurst: Senator Deuell, for what purpose?

Deuell: I've waited until Senator Davis finished the part she was talking about, fetal pain and she's gone on to another subject, so I'd like to ask her now, if she'll allow me some questions?

Davis: Not at this time, Mr. President, I'd like to continue please.

Deuell: Would the President ask Senator Davis when she plans on taking more questions?

Dewhurst: Senator Davis, do you have an idea when you might take questions?

Davis: I'm not sure, I'd like to at least finish the bill analysis and going through that, before I do.

Warren: Mr. President?

Dewhurst: Senator Warren, for what purpose?

Warren: Parliamentary inquiry.

Dewhurst: What do you inquire?

Warren: Is Senator Davis required to take questions when she has the floor?

Dewhurst: I'm advised by the Parliamentarian that she is not.

Warren: Thank you Mr. President.

Deuell: Mr. President, I might point out that taking questions for members is part of a long-standing Senate tradition. Thank you. [*Laughter.*]

Dewhurst: Senator Davis, you are recognized to continue.

Davis: Thank you. According to the bill analysis, many women suffer from minor to severe medical complications as a result of surgical procedures, including abortions. Women who choose to have an abortion should receive the same standard of care any other individual in Texas receives, regardless of the surgical procedure performed. The Committee Substitute to Senate Bill 5 seeks to increase the health and safety of a woman who chooses to have an abortion by requiring a physician performing or inducing an abortion to have admitting privileges at a hospital and to provide certain information to the woman. Now again, this is an issue a number of us on the Senate floor believe does not create a greater state of wellbeing and care for women who have had an abortion procedure. Requiring that a physician performing or inducing the abortion to have admitting privileges at a hospital and to provide certain information to the woman, in reality does two things; first of all, it decrease the number of doctors who would be able to provide this service to women, and unfortunately, by decreasing the number of doctors who would be qualified to provide this support, we are, actually, if such a provision were to pass into law, creating a situation where women actually would be subjected to what we all talked about earlier: the less safe procedures which returns to doctors who are not licensed under the law to perform abortions because they do not fit a particular legal criteria, and unfortunately the outgrowth of doctors who may begin to perform these services outside the law that might take us back to that point in time that once existed, not only in the state of Texas but in the country as a whole, where women subjected themselves to the medical care of someone who was less than competent to provide that care. The Committee Substitute to Senate Bill 5 also states that that physician has to provide certain information to the woman. And the information that we have received from TMA and from the obstetrics and gynecological group have all indicated to us that requiring a certain communication between a doctor and her patient is in controversy or, in, contravenes the typical law in Texas, as it relates to respecting the doctor-patient privilege. The bill analysis goes on to say, that in 1992 the Supreme Court ruled in *Casey vs. Planned Parenthood* that states have the right to regulate abortion clinics. In 1997 Texas enforced increased regulations. However, according to the bill analysis, today 38 licensed abortion facilities still operate at a second lower standard for the most common surgical procedure in Texas performed solely on women. Six Texas abortion facilities meet the standard as ambulatory surgical facilities, and I think we've had some differing information on that, some people say there are five that meet the standard, some people say that there are six. And again of course we've had the conversation about whether that standard actually creates an enhanced safety for women, and I actually have what Senator Deuell referenced a little while ago, a side by side comparison of what's required in each of those facilities so we can discuss that, and make a determination about the differences between those, and whether indeed it is the case that ambulatory surgical centers actually provide, through the licensing requirements, a greater standard of care for women in the state of Texas. But I wanna finish the bill analysis before I do that.

In medical practice Medicare is the national standard for insurance reimbursement. Abortion is an all cash or limited credit card business, so abortion facilities have not been subject to the same oversight as other surgical facilities. Moving abortion clinics under the guidelines for ambulatory surgical centers, according to the bill analysis, will provide Texas women choosing abortion the highest standard of care, of healthcare. Texas allows no other procedure to opt out of the accepted standard of care. Miscarriages are excluded from the definition of abortion as defined in section 245.002 of the Texas health and safety code. Physicians, offices and clinics performing less than fifty abortions in any 12-month period are excluded by section 245.004 of the Texas health and safety code. Committee Substitute to Senate Bill 5 amends chapter 171 of the health and safety code, to prohibit abortions at or after 20 weeks post fertilization, unless there is a significant physical threat to the life of the mother, amends current law relating to requirements for physicians who perform abortions, and creates an offense, amends current law relating to distributing or prescribing abortion inducing drugs, and provides penalties, and amends current law relating to minimum standards for abortion facilities. Committee Substitute for Senate Bill 5 amends current law relating to the regulation of abortion procedures, providers and facilities, and provides penalties. Now the bill analysis contains a, a note, a side note, while the statutory reference in this bill is to the Texas Department of Health, and the Texas Board of Health, the following amendments apt—affect the executive commissioner of the health and human services, and the department of state health services, as the successor agencies to TDH and the board. Then it sets out the rule-making authority. Rule-making authority previously granted to the Texas Board of Health is modified in section 4, section 245.010 health and safety code of this bill.

Now the section by section analysis of the bill: Section 1A provides that the findings indicate, that number one, substantial medical evidence recognizes that an unborn child is capable of experiencing pain by not later than 20 weeks after fertilization. And members I have a stack of articles that refute that there is substantial medical evidence that demonstrates that. And in fact I don't believe that as a member of the Senate I have been provided with information that demonstrates that substantial medical evidence. Uh, number two, the section A provides that the findings indicate, again we don't know whose these whose findings these are, the "findings" indicate that the state has a compelling state interest in protecting the lives of unborn children from the stage at which substantial medical evidence indicates that these children are capable of feeling pain.

Now you heard Senator Watson and I having a conversation about compelling state interests, and there is a reason that the bill analysis and the bill discuss and lay out this compelling state interest. And they do so in an attempt to protect the law, if it were to go into law, from a constitutional challenge under the provisions of *Roe v. Wade*, which of course created a standard that strict scrutiny should be the review by which any actions by a state in legislating restrictions on abortions should be met. And only under a strict scrutiny standard, where substantial or a compelling state interest can be demonstrated, can that strict scrutiny be met. Simply to say that it's so, in the bill analysis, members, and simply to say that it's so, in the bill itself, does not create a compelling state interest. And it's very interesting, actually, uh, this, and I'll go back to it again, the bill provides that "the findings indicate," and then there are no cited findings that demonstrate an indication of this "compelling" state interest, not a single one is mentioned in the bill. Instead, from somewhere on high, again we don't know from whom, "the findings indicate." We actually know that there is substantial medical evidence that demonstrates otherwise.

The section A3 also provides that "the findings indicate" that the "compelling state interest in protecting the lives of unborn children from the stage at which substantial medical evidence indicates that an unborn child is capable of feeling pain," is intended to be separate from and independent of the compelling state interests in protecting the lives of unborn children from the stage of viability, and neither state interest is intended to replace the other. Now that's kind of a belt and suspenders, members, that's put on to make sure that the state doesn't lose somehow its ability to argue that it has "a compelling state interest" in protecting a fetus after it is viable. And that simply by putting this 20-week pain provision in the bill, the state wants to make it clear that it's not giving up its other argument, that it has a substantial and "compelling state interest" in the viability in protecting a child from viability. In a way that's rather interesting, because it's very clear that the state is unable, the bill's authors are unable, to make the argument that the 20-week point of gestation is a viability point. And the authors were very careful to make sure to preserve viability as a protected and "compelling state interest."

Under section 4 of subsection A, restrictive elective abortions at or later than 20 weeks post-fertilization as provided by the fact, does not impose an undue burden or a substantial obstacle on a woman's ability to have an abortion. Now the reason that's set out, again under constitutional law as it's developed post *Roe v. Wade*, is that the state must demonstrate that it's not imposing an undue burden, or a substantial obstacle on a woman's ability to have a legal abortion. And again this is a finding, "the findings indicate that," this doesn't occur. But I think there's certainly an argument that can be made, that indeed this does impose an undue burden, and that indeed it is a substantial obstacle on a woman's ability to have an abortion. And of course, were this to become law, that will be an argument most certainly made by proponents who believe that this law is in violation of the constitution. This provides that the reason it's not an undue burden is two-fold. One, because the woman has adequate time to decide whether to have an abortion in the first 20 weeks after fertilization. And Members, we've heard some stories from testimony, women who routinely have missed periods, they have menstrual cycles that are not reliable and sometimes it actually is later than 20 weeks when a woman discovers that she's pregnant. We've also heard that sometimes medical treatments that a woman is receiving can interfere with that cycle and, and also throw her into a situation where she doesn't understand by virtue of a missed period that she is pregnant until beyond this time. And of course we also know, as has been provided in multiple evidence to us on this bill, that sometimes fetal abnormalities, in fact many times, are not discovered until after this point in time. The other reason that, uh, the section by section analysis indicates that this would not impose an undue burden or a substantial obstacle on a woman's ability to have an abortion, is because the act does not apply to abortions that are necessary to avert the death, or substantial and irreversible physical impairment of a major bodily function of the pregnant woman.

Now we know, we've been hearin' it from the medical community, that they feel that this puts them in a terrible position. Because in order not to violate this law and to be subject to penalties under this law, doctors would have to approve, they would have to prove, that the abortion post 20 weeks was necessary to avert the death, or substantial and irreversible physical impairment of a major bodily function of a pregnant woman. And as you can imagine, reasonable minds could likely disagree on this issue. And what's the likely outcome of this particular provision will be, is that women who seek a post–20-week abortion may be unable to find a doctor who's willing to take this risk, even if she is undergoing some substantial medical harm that might occur to her, a doctor may not want to be the decider as to whether this would be necessary to avert death, or substantial and irreversible physical impairment of a major bodily function. There hasn't been any case law developed on that yet. And most doctors are not going to want to take that risk. And if we do care about making sure that we're not subjecting doctors to unnecessary risks, we certainly would wanna make sure that we gave thought and care to that particular provision, and at the very least exempt doctors from any kind of penalty that they violate that, but that is not the case. There is a penalty for a doctor who violates this particular provision and I'll, I'll get to that in the bill analysis in a moment.

There's a subsection B that provides that the legislature intends that every application of this statute to every individual woman be severable from each other. It requires that the application of the statute to those women, in the unexpected event that the application of this statute is found to impose an impermissible undue burden on any pregnant woman or group of pregnant women, be severed from the remaining applications of the statute that do not impose an undue burden, and those remaining applications are required to remain enforced and unaffected consistent with section ten of the fact. Now again, not atypical for a, a bill to have a severability clause in it, um, and that's another belt and suspenders item that's included so that if there were a portion of this bill that some women were successful in demonstrating actually did not meet the constitutional standards that it's meant to, to meet, if some women were able to demonstrate that, this an attempt by the author of the bill to sever that finding from an impact that it would have on other decisions that may be made under this bill, and to different women under different circumstances.

Section 2 in the bill analysis amends subchapter A, chapter 171 of the health and safety code by adding 171.0031 as follows: section 171.0031 is titled "Requirements of Physician Offense," this is what I was talking about a moment ago, the offences that physicians will be subject to if they are found to have violated provisions of this particular area of the bill. Subsection A requires a physician performing or inducing an abortion to number one, on the date the abortion is performed, have active admitting privileges at a hospital that is located not further than 30 miles from the location at which the abortion is performed or induced, and provides obstetrical or gynecological health-care services. So let's break that down. On the date that the abortion is performed this has to be in place. The doctor must have active admitting privileges at a hospital, and that means the doctor needs to, on active basis, be participating in providing care, medical care, at the hospital. A question was asked a moment ago, "Well why wouldn't a doctor go ahead and just get admitting privileges, and then continue to be able to provide these services?" Well I have two responses to that. Number one, because this requires that the doctor have active admitting privileges, and if a doctor doesn't practice medicine in a hospital facility, like doctor Campbell does in the ER, then a doctor isn't going to have these active admitting privileges. And to require that they be active, not just that there be an admitting privilege, but to require that they be active as this bill does, serves the very purpose that many of, of us are concerned that it serves. It serves the purpose that doctors, fewer, far fewer doctors, would be provided with the capacity under the law, to provide what today they are providing in legal, safe clinical settings to women. And actually it would be very interesting to know, and I don't know if anyone's done this analysis yet, how many fewer doctors would there be who would satisfy the provisions of this ordinance, and therefore be able to practice medicine in abortion clinics were this particular provision to go in place? And would hospitals somehow then feel pressured to create admitting privileges, active admitting privileges, and how would they handle that? Of course we got a letter from THA that spoke directly to that, and, and, and they said ya know we, we reserve the right to grant admitting privileges to doctors who practice in the areas that we need them to practicing in our hospital. Most of them don't have the need for doctors who perform abortion services as active admitted, admitting privileges doctors for their hospital. And I think the bill authors understand that, that at the end of the day what this is going to do is create fewer and fewer options for women to exercise their constitutional right. Now the fact that it has to be located not further than 30 miles from the abortion facility, again I, I don't know if anyone's done the analysis on this yet, but I'd be really curious to know how many of the existing abortion facilities are within 30 miles from a, a hospital where a doctor could be licensed. In fact, I'd be interested to know of the ambulatory surgical centers, would that actually disqualify any of them even under this bill, if a doctor who practiced in that ambulatory surgical center didn't have a hospital even within 30 miles to which he or she could gain active admitting privileges. What's that going to do in terms of the number of facilities that would qualify here? And what I, what I found that's really interesting about that too, and we talked about this in debate on the bill, was, there are so many ambulatory surgical centers I, I've got a list of them here, I, I may read that in a minute, there's a long list of them, that only five, or maybe six, actually perform abortion services at them. And, and what we wondered out loud when we debated this bill on the floor was, ya know if what we really care about is that abortions take place in ambulatory surgical centers, why don't we require ambulatory surgical centers to provide that service? Here we're providing, we're, we're requiring the hospitals do something. We're requiring that if they have an interest in making sure that abortion services can continue to exist in an area in which they reside, that they will have to admit these physicians as active admitted physicians, we're, we're actually imposing a legislative requirement on hospitals to do that. But we're not imposing any kind of requirement on ambulatory surgical centers to allow these procedures, and if what we really cared about was women's safety and wellbeing, why wouldn't we think about doing that? There are, there are many, many, many, uh, surgical centers, ambulatory surgical centers that fit this bill.

The other requirement of the physician in an offence if the physician does not meet it, is that the physician must provide the pregnant woman with a telephone number by which the pregnant woman may reach the physician, or other healthcare personnel employed by the physician, or by the facility at which the abortion was performed with access to the woman's relevant medical records, 24 hours a day to request assistance for any complications that arise from the performance of the abortion, or ask health-related questions regarding the abortion. Now I talked about that requirement a moment ago, and I think that most people would agree, that if a woman has had an abortion, and there may be complications that arise, I used the example a while ago when I had my wisdom teeth out, my dentist made sure that I had his number, that I could call him in the next 24 hours even if it was twelve o'clock at night, if, if I had some excess bleeding. He also gave me the phone number of someone who worked in his dental office if I couldn't reach him. And I don't think any of us would disagree, that a woman who's had an abortion should be provided with information in the event that something happens after she leaves the facility. Of course it's the practice of the facilities right now for women to wait for a certain period of time for them to determine that she is ok and, and ready to be released. But certainly I think we could all agree if, if this were the provision of the bill, if this were it, if we were truly talking about women's healthcare, if we were truly talking about making sure women were safe after an abortion, this is the kind of thing that goes right to the heart of that and that we could agree should happen.

The other thing that the woman must be provided with, according to the bill analysis, is the name and the telephone number of the nearest hospital to the home of the pregnant woman. Now let's, let's think about that for a minute. It's not the nearest hospital to the abortion facility, it's not the hospital within 30 miles of the abortion facility, it's that the woman be given the telephone number of the nearest hospital to her home. And remember members when we debated this bill, and we talked about that woman from Laredo whose returned home, if she has a complication that arises, and she's driven the 200 miles to San Antonio to one of the only ambulatory surgical centers that provides abortion services in the state of Texas, and she gets all the way back to Laredo, she's not gonna go to a hospital that's 30 miles from the abortion facility, she's gonna go to a hospital near her home. And it's another indicator of why it makes absolutely no sense for the doctor who performed her abortion to have admitting privileges at a hospital that's 30 miles away from the facility, when even the bill itself says the doctor, the abortion facility's not supposed to give the woman the name and the address of the hospital that's 30 miles away from the facility, he's supposed to give her the name and the telephone number of the nearest hospital to her home.

Under subsection B, it provides that a physician who violates subsection A commits an offence and provides that under this section it's a class A misdemeanor, punishable only by a fine, but it's a class A misdemeanor, it's a crime, members, for a doctor to fail to have privileges at a hospital within 30 miles of an abortion facility, and a failure for the doctor to provide the information that's required, and that I think we all agree should be required. Section 3 amends chapter 171 of the health and safety code, by adding subchapters C and D as follows. Subchapter C: abortion prohibited at or after 20 weeks post fertilization. Section 171.041 short title, authorizes that this subchapter be cited as the Pre-born Pain Act, wants to make sure that that title is provided to this particular provision of the law, the Pre-born Pain Act. Again, because that's used, that's argued as the "compelling state interest," for which this 20-week pain provision is being required, or being prohibited, excuse me, the 20-week abortion. In the definitions it defines pre-fertilization age and severe fetal abnormality in the chapter.

So let's talk about the fertilization age issue. Section 171.043 requires a determination of post-fertilization age. And it prohibits a physician, except as otherwise provided by section 171.046, from performing or inducing, or attempting to perform or induce, an abortion without first making a determination of the probable post-fertilization age of the unborn child. Now let's think about that for a minute. We're going to hold doctors to a very difficult standard here. We're going to ask doctors to make a determination of the probable post-fertilization age of the fetus. Now, members, we've all gotten a lot of information from the medical community on this particular issue. And what they tell us is, this isn't the standard that's used, it's, it's never been the standard that's used, because it's an impossible standard to meet, because it's asking doctors to do something that they are incapable of doing. Unless a woman becomes impregnated by in vitro fertilization, well, then they can tell you the probable post-fertilization age of a fetus. But doctors use a different standard for determining gestational age, and they do it for a reason. They do it because it's the most reliable, and they do it because they have absolutely no idea exactly when fertilization occurs, because for every woman, her ovulation period is different. Some women actually ovulate during their menstrual cycle and get pregnant when they think they can't get pregnant . . . during their menstrual cycle, because they're ovulating during that period of time. And there is a reason that fertilization is not the standard that's used because, members, doctors have a better understanding of how to judge gestational age than a bunch of senators from the State of Texas do. But we're gonna tell them, by golly, that they can't even . . .

Dewhurst: Senator Estes, for what purpose do you rise?

Estes: Parliamentary inquiry.

Dewhurst: So state your . . .

Estes: I've been looking at rule 6.13, it says when a reading of papers is called for and the same is objected by any member it shall be determined by a majority vote of the senate without debate. Is it appropriate to make a parliamentary inquiry about the reading of papers in this filibuster?

Dewhurst: You are recognized.

Estes: A little bit later on it says the senator addressing the senate . . . this is in the rulings . . . on the question of whether or not the senate shall concur, in the House amendments to a bill may read in full the legal opinion relating to the subject matter of the amendments unless the senate orders the reading discontinued. Is that correct?

Dewhurst: That is correct.

Estes: Thank you, Mr. President.

Dewhurst: Senator Davis, you are recognized.

Davis: Thank you, Mr. President.

Zaffirini: Mr. President . . . Mr. President?

Dewhurst: Senator Zaffirini, for what purpose do you rise?

Zaffirini: For a point of information, Mr. President.

Dewhurst: You are re . . .

Zaffirini: Thank you, some of us did not hear Senator Estes' question and your answer; would you mind repeating it for us, please?

[*Pause.*]

Dewhurst: I didn't make a ruling, did not make a ruling, but . . . Senator Estes is asking about rule 6.13, when a reading of the papers is called for and the same is objected to by any member, it shall be determined by a majority vote of the senate, and without debate. I think what Senator Estes was asking is that if the senate . . . if a senator objects to the reading of documents and the senate votes, that the senator shall stop reading from that document.

Zaffirini: Thank you, Mr. President; I have another point of information.

Dewhurst: You are recognized.

Zaffirini: Thank you, Mr. President. Senator Van de Putte has arrived, and my question is at what point will we consider the resolution honoring her father?

Dewhurst: Later this evening.

Zaffirini: Later this evening? Thank you.

Dewhurst: Senator Watson, for what purpose . . .

Watson: Parliamentary inquiry.

Dewhurst: State your inquiry.

Watson: With regard to rule 6.13 entitled "Dispense With Reading of Papers," if in fact there is an objection by a member and it is determined by a majority vote of the senate, I suppose the determination would be that the paper can't be read. Is that correct?

Dewhurst: Senator, that is correct. If the members vote to . . .

Watson: Parliamentary inquiry, Mr. President.

Dewhurst: State your inquiry.

Watson: If the senate were to vote that the papers could not be read, that would not be a strike . . . a warning or a strike that would lead to a determination by the senate about whether the filibuster goes on, is that correct?

Dewhurst: Senator, I'm advised by the Parliamentarian that not on the first case, but if she continued to read different documents it would be.

Watson: But for clarity purposes: there would have to be an objection to the reading of papers . . .

Dewhurst: That is correct.

Watson: . . . there would have to be . . .

Dewhurst: A vote.

Watson: . . . a vote, I suppose it would be subject to a debate, as to whether or not . . . it would be a straight vote, and that would not be a strike unless there were continued issues?

Dewhurst: That is correct.

Watson: Thank you, Mr. President.

Dewhurst: Senator Ellis, for what purpose?

Ellis: Parliamentary inquiry, Mr. President.

Dewhurst: State your inquiry.

Ellis: This rule, 6.13, relates to the reading of a paper. My inquiry is, is a member who is conducting a filibuster permitted to read from a computer, or to read from an iPad? This specifically says, "When a reading of a *paper* is called," so my question is, is a senator permitted to read from something other than paper? It specifically says "paper" in the rule-book. Since we have a strict conformity with the rules, it does say "paper," Mr. President, not a computer. [*Crosstalk.*]

Dewhurst: Senator Ellis, our rules were written a number of years ago, the meaning of the word "paper" would include reading from printed documents, whether they're on your computer, or you have them in hard copy right in front of you.

Ellis: Thank you, Mr. President. Another parliamentary inquiry?

Dewhurst: State your inquiry.

Ellis: Is it fair to say that these rules have become very flexible in this body?

Dewhurst: I don't think that's a proper inquiry.

Ellis: Ok, thank you, Mr. President.

Dewhurst: Senator West, for what purpose do you rise, sir?

West: I just want to make sure I understand the rule, first of all. Let me, Let me make sure I read it right, and if I'm wrong, someone let me know. "When the reading of a paper is called for." So, this rule would only apply if the reading of the paper was called for initially, right? [*Extended pause. Crosstalk.*]

Dewhurst: Senator West, it's my understanding that when Senator Estes made his inquiry, he was referring to rule 6.13 . . .

West: Correct.

Dewhurst: . . . but he was referring to a specific ruling that says, "A senator addressing the senate . . . A senator addressing the senate on a question of whether or not the senate shall concur in the House amendments to a bill, may read in full a legal opinion relating to the subject matter of the paper of the amendments, unless the senate orders its reading discontinued."

West: So, alright, so then is it . . . then is it, do we just limit that to the facts, and the facts being "a legal opinion," or is it um to be construed more broadly than that? Because the rule specifically says that when the reading of a paper is called for, and the same is objected to by members. So it looks like, at least based on the rules that we passed, ok, the reading has to be called for and the same objected to by a member. That's what the rule says; now . . . that's what the that's what the black and white letter of the rule that we passed at the beginning of the session. When the reading of a paper is called for and the same is objected to by any member, it shall be determined by the majority vote of the senate without debate. And I'm just trying to figure out, in this instance, what reading was called for, for purposes of its applicability to the filibuster that's being . . .

Dewhurst: Senator, let's address . . . if you'll come forward I'll address it with you. [*Extended pause. Crosstalk.*]

Dewhurst: Members, we're going to move forward. Senator Davis has the floor.

Davis: Thank you, Mr. President. Now, I'm going through this bill analysis bit by bit because I have something to say about all of it, and I want to make sure that the public understands exactly what the provisions of this bill require. We were just having a conversation about post-fertilization age, and that the physician is required under the terms of this bill to determine post-fertilization age, and the physician can then only perform or induce, or attempt to perform or induce an abortion, once he or she has determined that the fetus is 20 weeks or less from fertilization. And I, and I, I, I wanna make the point about the incalculability of that, and what we are subjecting doctors to. And if we say to doctors from this point forward that that's the starting point, how in the world are they ever going to make that determination? And to be on the safe side, let's face it, the way they're going to make the determination is they're gonna over-correct, and it's very likely that in the over-correct, women who are 18 months . . . or excuse me, 18 weeks, gestational age of their fetus, those women will have a very hard time finding a doctor who doesn't want to risk violating this, because the doctor can't be clear about the 20-million-dollar question of when fertilization occurs. Now, a doctor can rely . . . which is kind of interesting . . . under the bill, they can rely on the determination of that post-fertilization that another doctor has done. And so now, now we're gonna have two of them involved. So, now we're gonna ask . . . and I just don't see that this will ever occur . . . that one doctor's willing to say to another doctor, "You know what, fertilization occurred on November the eighth, and therefore, 20 weeks from November the eighth is X." That's physician A. And then physician B says, "Well, I was relying on what physician A told me." So, now we've got two of them who potentially have a problem. What if physician A says, "I didn't say that, I was talking about the date of the last menstrual cycle, I was talking about the date of the woman's last period . . . I wasn't talking about, fertilization. How am I supposed to know when fertilization occurs?" And what we know, members, by doing this, is we are subjecting doctors to a requirement that they cannot meet. And we're asking them to put their practices essentially on the line if they make a mistake. So, in the grand scheme of what we've been talking about here, and the impact on women in Texas, there are so many people who say, "This isn't gonna limit women's ability to have abortions in the state of Texas." Well, yes, it is. Because every single one of the pieces of this legislation that I've been talking about adds up to a sum, and that sum is one that creates a greater and greater and greater challenge to women in the state of Texas to do what? To exercise her constitutional protected right to have an abortion, to exercise the most difficult decision of her life.

And Members . . . we've, we've all heard from these witnesses. I read from so many of them today, you heard their testimony in committee, we've heard them before; we heard them when we were taking up the sonogram bill last session. And we know that women can find themselves in situations where the provisions of this bill are going to create true hardships for them. And you heard it in some of the letters; a lot of women really resent the fact that this legislating is being done and voted on, look around the room, primarily by men. And yes, there were a few women over in the senate side, and a few over in the house side, that supported this bill, but you can imagine . . . or maybe you can't . . . how a woman feels to be told that her feelings on these issues, that no matter how difficult, no matter the circumstance that she's dealing with, if she can't fit into every one of these little square pegs, that she's going to be asked to be fit into by this bill, she is not going to be able to exercise her constitutional rights. And what's so disturbing is that we don't seem to care. And maybe that is because so many of us on this floor have never, ever had to face that, and never will face it, because you don't have the equipment. And I've got it, and my daughters have it, and other women that I care about have it, and women who I don't know have it; and what I know for a fact is that each of them has a unique circumstance that's going to be impacted directly by virtue of the provisions in this particular bill.

Senator Deuell: Mr. President?

Dewhurst: Senator Deuell, for what purpose do you rise?

Deuell: To ask Senator Davis some questions, would she yield?

Dewhurst: Senator Davis, do you yield?

Davis: I'm not yielding for any questions at this point, thank you.

Dewhurst: Senator Deuell, Senator does not yield. Senator Nelson for what purpose . . .

Nelson: Well, I was going to ask if the gentlelady would yield.

Davis: I don't wish to yield for a question at this time.

Nelson: Mr. President, may I ask the gentlelady if there is any point this evening that she will yield for some questions from another woman?

Davis: I, I may do that, but I, I am not yielding for a question at this time.

Nelson: Thank you, Mr. President.

Dewhurst: Floor is yours, Senator Davis.

Davis: Thank you, Mr. President. Now, the prohibition in this bill says that a doctor can't perform or induce, or attempt to perform or induce an abortion on a woman if it's determined, as we said a moment ago, that the fetus is 20 or more weeks post-fertilization; we've already talked about how difficult that is. But then there's a, a provision in here about the method of abortion. And again, this implies or, or, or puts in place a requirement that physicians function from a post-fertilization age perspective when applying the provisions of this particular piece of the bill. But it does say that there are exceptions, and it provides that the prohibitions and the requirements under the bill in all the sections thus far that I've referred to, do not apply if there exists a condition that in the physician's reasonable medical judgment would so complicate the medical condition of the woman, to avert the woman's death or a serious risk of substantial and irreversible physical impairment of a major bodily function. Now, we talked about that. So now there's an exception to this 20-week bill. There's an exception. And the exception puts a doctor, once again, in a very precarious situation, because it provides that the doctor, number one, using reasonable medical judgment. So, we're in the trial, and I can just tell you how that goes, the first thing that happens is the jury or the judge is gonna have to decide what was "reasonable medical judgment." And what's interesting about that is, often times, you've got a lot of people that don't really know what "reasonable medical judgment" is; you of course call experts to the stand, and they talk about what might be reasonable and what wasn't reasonable, and juries have to put themselves in the mind of a medical professional and they have to decide what is "reasonable medical judgment." But then they've also got to decide, was that judgment reasonable in relation to other terms that are fairly subjective in nature, and require . . . and I think differing minds would agree . . . when these conditions are met. The conditions are this: that in the physician's reasonable medical judgment, failing to provide this service, this post–20-week abortion, would so complicate the medical condition of a woman, that to avert her death or a serious risk of substantial and irreversible physical impairment of a major bodily function must be demonstrated.

Now, I wonder what that means. Irreversible physical impairment of a major bodily function. I've been pregnant. I'm sure a lot of women here and in the gallery have been pregnant, and we've probably had changes in our bodies that have occurred as a consequence of that. Some of us might refer to them as physical impairments. For many women, I hate to be graphic, but for many women who've carried a, a child, she has problems hold—holding her bladder, she has problems with urination. I wonder if a jury would think about that as being a physical impairment. I wonder what a jury might decide was a irreversible, physical impairment that justified a doctor using "reasonable medical judgment" to avert. What might that be? And there's no guidance, there's no guidance in the bill analysis, there's no guidance In the bill itself, as to what that might be. And does it make you pause for a moment and consider why the medical community has so many concerns about this bill? What are they subjecting themselves to? And, and will doctors continue to practice in this arena? We talked a, a lot about that before I was here but it was a major part of the conversation in deciding whether we should move forward with tort reform, part of the argument being that when doctors feel like they are subjected to unreasonable risks, they will not practice in that arena. On the tort reform arena, the arena, was the state of Texas, and there was argument made and information put forward that doctors were leaving the state of Texas or if they had gone to residency school somewhere they weren't coming back to the state of Texas, because they worried that they couldn't practice here without subjecting themselves to unreasonable risk. Could that perhaps be the purpose of legislation like this? Could perhaps a justification, a, a motive for legislation like this be in any way related to having physicians think twice about practicing in this area of medicine? Could it be that in Texas, what the hoped for outcome would be that fewer and fewer doctors practice in this area of medicine? And, as a doctor, I wonder what they think about that particular piece of this and as things advance, I wonder how many will be willing to take these risks? Now there's also a provision here that protects privacy in court proceedings. And it's a, it's a good protection I think. It's assuring that in a laundry list of litigation that I have just gone though in the last hour, that when that litigation occurs whether it's in a criminal court of law or a civil court of law, the woman would have her identity protected and not subject to public disclosure if she does not consent to giving that disclosure and, and there's a, a greater protection here requiring the court to issue orders to the parties that this protection would be in place . . . to witnesses, and to the counsel, that they aren't to reveal outside the courtroom a woman's identity who may be a subject of a proceeding where a doctor is actually having some challenges to provision of the medical care that they provided. And then there is some provision that would authorize the court to disclose that information in certain circumstances. Number one, if a motion is filed with the court requesting it, if notice of that motion is served on each interested party, and if the court determines the disclosure is essential to the administration of justice and there is no reasonable alternative to disclosure. Now, what does that mean? When might a court find that disclosing the identity of a woman who's had a very traumatic procedure and who's gone through the personal pain and the scarring of having undergone that procedure, when might it be the case that that woman, her identity, would be disclosed because it would be deemed essential to the administration of justice and that there is no reasonable alternative to that disclosure? Might that have a chilling effect? Could that be the hoped-for impact?

Now, there's another section in the bill about the abortion-inducing drugs and I see that Senator Van de Putte has joined the body this evening. We're so happy to have Senator Van de Putte on the floor and we, of course, all share in the pain she's going through right now. She did a great job the other day on abortion-inducing drugs, and, and talking about the way the bill is written and from her perspective as a pharmacist why the way the terms of this provision are written, can actually put women in harm's way. Now let's go back to that original intent that we talked about of this bill: to protect women's health. That's not what the Twitter said, the Tweet, but that's what we said here on the Senate floor—to protect women's health. And Senator Van de Putte made some excellent points about the fact that there is now a very tightly defined administration of abortion-inducing drugs that will occur as a consequence of this particular bill if it's to go into law. It provides enforcement through the Texas Medical Board. And it requires the Texas Medical Board, interestingly enough, a Board that is made up of physicians, to . . . regulate

Dewhurst: Senator Davis, if you'll excuse me for a moment. Senator Campbell, for what purpose do you rise?

Senator Campbell: Will the gentlewoman yield for questions?

Davis: I'll, I'll not yield at this time. Thank you, Mr. President.

Dewhurst: Senator Davis declines to yield.

Campbell: Um, even to a female and a physician?

Dewhurst: Uh, the Senator has declined to yield.

Campbell: Thank you, Mr. President. Thank you for your consideration.

Dewhurst: Thank you, Senator Campbell. Senator Davis . . .

Davis: Thank you, Mr. President. Now the, as I was saying, the, the Texas Medical Board is charged with actually enforcing this and, and the interesting thing about it is the requirements in the bill here fly completely in the face of what typically happens in the medical arena in the administration of drugs. Now what typically happens is, a, a drug is approved by the FDA, and doctors administer it, perhaps initially, according to the label. And as they experience the impacts of that drug on their patient community, they find that the label actually isn't creating administration that provides the best care for their patient, in the administration of that drug. They also sometimes find that drugs can be used in off-label uses, as the saying goes, of, for example, I think Senator Van de Putte gave us the example, of aspirin. We used to think, you know, that you take aspirin if you have a fever. Take aspirin if you had a headache. I think that's what the label says. But now, we know that doctors tell people who are at risk of heart disease and stroke, that it's a good idea to chew a baby aspirin, every single day. A baby aspirin a day, keeps the heart attack away. And, of course, medical professionals know this. And what medical professionals have learned about this particular drug, and the point that Senator Van de Putte made so well, is that this particular drug, if administered according to the label, and according to the FDA prescribed recommendations for its use, actually have resulted in creating problems for women, have actually created in greater uterine bleeding, and actually have put women at greater risk because the dosages were higher on the label, and by the FDA recommendation, than doctors learned in their experience was really needed to provide the woman with a safe abortion procedure. And, what doctors also learned was the administration of the drug, not just the amount of drug to be given, actually made a difference in terms of the well-being of women, depending on whether it was administered orally or vaginally. And I read something earlier about that, that talked about the fact that a lower dose in that first dose, I think it's about a third lower than what the label and what the FDA requirement says should be given, and then on the second day, that the second dose, again a lower dose, should be given vaginally, not orally, and that the outcomes for their patients, are far better when they do that. But the legislature has decided in its all-knowingness to change that, and to subject physicians to standards that they know are not in the best interest of their patients. And then not only are they doing that, but they require the Texas Medical Board to enforce it, a Texas Medical Board, made of up doctors, who probably know that this is not in keeping with good medical practice, but their legislators told them that they have to enforce it. That's going to be a really interesting enforcement action if it causes action against a doctor is brought before the Texas Medical Board. And, and, and let's talk about exactly what legislators in their wisdom have decided in place of what doctors have decided in terms of the administration of this drug. First of all, it requires that the physician before he or she gives or sells or dispenses, administers, provides, or prescribes the drug to examine the pregnant woman and document in her medical record, the gestational age and intrauterine location of the pregnancy. Now, interestingly, here, when it says gestational age, it doesn't refer to fertilization date. So, if I'm a doctor, and other parts of the bill say I've got to document fetal age based on fertilization date, but this particular section of the bill doesn't address that, what if I put the date as being something that's relative to the woman's last menstrual cycle? Am I violating a provision of this law—unknowingly, accidentally? Because it doesn't really speak to it in this section, it only speaks to it in that previous section that I was talking about. It requires that the physician who gives or sells or dispenses those medicines to provide the pregnant woman with, now this is interesting, a copy of the final printed label of the drug. So, I'm gonna give, Susan, a label. Now, I don't know about you, but when I buy an over-the-counter drug, I read the label and then I take the drug according to the label. And so if my doctor now is required not just to give me a prescription where I go to the drug store and I pick it up and on it are written the doctor's orders for when I'm supposed to take it, but instead, what I gotta get now, what the doctor has to give me is "the label." And the label, thanks to the great information provided to us by our pharmacist, Senator Van de Putte, the label actually tells the woman to do something that physicians have learned not to be in her best health and safety interest. But she's going to have that label now, and if the doctor tells her to take it otherwise, she's probably going to question that. Which should she do? Well then, in case she has any questions, according to the bill, the physician also has to give the pregnant woman a telephone number so that she can reach her doctor or other healthcare personnel employed by the physician, at which the abortion was performed. Now, that's kind of interesting. Uh, I'd have a, I'd have an interesting time with that as a lawyer in a courtroom. The facility in which an abortion was performed when a woman is taking the drug, what's that drug called? Um, I had it here somewhere. RU486. It's my understanding, that an abortion that occurs as a consequence of taking that drug, doesn't happen when the woman takes it, in fact, she has to take two doses of it. And then typically it takes several days after the administration of that second dose for the abortion to occur. For her body, basically, to go into a labor that expels the fetus. So the doctor's got to give her a telephone number of healthcare personnel at which the abortion was performed. When is the abortion performed when you take RU486? It's kind of an interesting question, and again, I think it subjects doctors to some concerns about some lack of true direction and objectivity, objective direction, in the bill. Then it requires that the physician who gives or sells or dispenses, provides this abortion-inducing drug, to schedule a follow-up visit for the woman to occur not more than 14 days after the administration or use of the drug. Now, I read some testimony previously from doctors who have said, typically, the practice is that a woman doesn't go back to the abortion facility, instead she goes to her family doctor or her own OB-GYN in order to assure that everything went as it should have and that she's okay, and that she doesn't need any further medical care, in terms of completing that procedure. But this is going to require that the physician schedule a follow-up visit for the woman to occur not more than 14 days after the administration or use of the drug. Now, let's layer that upon that sonogram bill from last session. And remember that sonogram bill. There have been a lot of stories since it went into law about the hardship it's created for women who now have to go for a sonogram on one day and then return no less than 24 hours later on the second day. There have been instances . . .

Campbell: Mr. President

Davis: Where women have had . . .

Campbell: Mr. President.

Davis: Some real hardship because they've shown up on the second day . . .

Campbell: Mr. President.

Davis: And the same doctor is not there . . .

Dewhurst: Senator Campbell, for what purpose do you rise?

Campbell: Um, a point of order, just to inquire about the subject matter at this moment.

Dewhurst: State your point of order.

Campbell: Um, I believe we are talking about, we're talking about the sonogram bill, and you know, doctors and sonogram bill, versus we are supposed to be—the last topic she was on was RU486. Are we still to remain to this bill? Because, um, an analogy to the sonogram bill is not specific to this bill.

Dewhurst: Would you please come to the platform and we will discuss this with the Parliamentarian?

Campbell: Yes, sir.

Davis: M, Mr. President . . .

Dewhurst: Senator Davis, would you like to address that point of order?

Davis: I would like to respond. I know ya'll are going to go up there and talk about it but I don't feel I can leave my little sphere here, but what I'm talking about is this bill layered upon a previous law that this legislature enacted and the further hardships that are created for women. And it's important in order for me to describe the impact of this particular bill and that's what I'm clearly talking about—the impact of this particular bill. I think it's perfectly reasonable to talk about it in the context of what women in Texas today will face if this provision goes in place. And that's why, of course, I was referring to the existing visit requirements.

Dewhurst: Thank you, Senator Davis. [*Extended pause.*]

Dewhurst: Members, after consultation with the Parliamentarian and after going over what, what people heard as far as discussion, Senator Campbell your point of order is well-taken and is sustained.

Gallery: [*Extended yelling, shouting.*] Bullshit! [*Increased yelling, shouting.*]

[*Various attempts to speak by members.*]

Dewhurst: Can you hear me? Senator Watson, can you hear me?

Gallery [*chanting*]: Let her speak! Let her speak! Let her speak! . . .

[*End filibuster.*]